Fascinating Snakes of Southeast Asia

– An Introduction

Fascinating Snakes
of Southeast Asia
– An Introduction

Francis Lim Leong Keng
Monty Lee Tat-Mong

Contents

Foreword by Dr Ong Swee Law **vii**

Foreword by Bernard Harrison **viii**

Preface **xi**

Acknowledgements and Photo credits **xiii**

List of Photographs Used in the Descriptions of Snakes **xv**

Introduction **1**

Snakes in Religions and Folklore **4**

Snake Encounters **8**

Snakes and Snakebites **13**

Some Fantastic Facts about Snakes **23**

Tropical Press Sdn. Bhd.
29, Jalan Riong, 59100 Kuala Lumpur,
Malaysia

First published 1989

ISBN 967-73-0045-8

Printed by Art Printing Works Sdn. Bhd.
29, Jalan Riong, 59100 Kuala Lumpur,
Malaysia

Perpustakaan Negara Malaysia   Data-Mengkatalog-dalam-Penerbitan

Lim, Francis Leong Keng
    Fascinating snakes of Southeast Asia :
    an introduction / Francis Lim Leong
    Keng, Monty Lee Tat-Mong.

    Bibliography: p.119–120
    ISBN 967–73–0045–8
    1. Snakes – Asia, Southeastern.
    I. Lee, Monty Tat-Mong. II. Title.
    597.960959

Overleaf: Common House Snake/Wolf Snake
Page i: Baby Rock Python

Pythons and Other Primitive Snakes **26**

Non-venomous Colubrine Snakes **36**

Back-fanged Mildly Venomous Snakes **62**

Front-fanged Venomous Snakes **82**

Appendix I – List of Snakes found in Peninsular Malaysia
(according to M.W.F.Tweedie, 1983) **109**

Appendix II – Distribution Chart & List of Common Names
of Snakes of Southeast Asia **115**

Bibliography **119**

Index **121**

Head of Mangrove Snake

Dedicated to
our children

Foreword

by Dr Ong Swee Law

Most people find snakes repulsive, whereas some find them attractive. Some people regard snakes as slimy, evil creatures; others find them clean and beautiful. Ecologists tell us that snakes help to keep the rodent population down, and gardeners will be pleased to learn that snakes eat insects which thrive on their plants. Mr Francis Lim Leong Keng, in his book, has endeavoured to dispel widespread ignorance of these fascinating members of the animal world, and it is both a pleasure and a privilege for me to write this foreword.

I recommend this book to all those who wish to learn about snakes as a first step towards undertaking a more detailed study of the subject. It will be especially useful to those who own a garden, or to picnickers, hikers, or members of the Armed Forces who may visit the more rural parts of Singapore. Encounters of the reptilian kind may take place, and it will be good to be armed with the knowledge this book provides of the many different species of snakes found in Singapore, Peninsular Malaysia as well as other parts of Southeast Asia. To be able to distinguish between the harmless and the venomous snakes, and to know how to treat snakebites could mean the difference between staying alive or being dead. It could also mean that harmless snakes are spared from being killed out of ignorance.

Mr Francis Lim belongs to a core of dedicated, competent keepers without whom a zoo cannot look after its animal stock effectively. He scored a distinction in the City & Guilds Certificate in Animal Management, winning the first prize award — a bronze medal — in March 1988 . His 14 years of working experience with our Zoo have been spent almost entirely with reptiles, thus qualifying him as an authority on this subject. Further evidence of his competence can be seen at the Reptile Garden in the Singapore Zoological Gardens, the design of which is partly the result of his contribution, and the care of its inmates solely his responsibility.

Executive Chairman
Singapore Zoological Gardens
30 June 1988

Foreword

by Bernard Harrison

It is most unfortunate that snakes have the reputation of being dangerous. This of course is true of some of the more venomous and the larger specimens of the constrictors, but the vast majority are harmless to man, and serve an important part in the ecological network. Their ecological role in Singapore, almost devoid of indigenous carnivorous mammals, is an important point, as all snakes are carnivores.

It may well be that the absence of limbs gives snakes a 'creepy' appearance. Generally, people do not mind having geckos crawling on their ceiling, but imagine how they would react on seeing a Common House Snake in the same situation!

It may also be the venom, possessed by a small percentage of snake species, which has instilled this almost paranoid reaction in most people when faced with a snake. The limbless appearance and possible danger snakes pose have made them become the most mis-understood, feared and persecuted group of animals in the world.

In both Hindu and Taoist cultures, snakes are revered. It is unfortunate that snakes have been portrayed as evil in Christian dogma, like the serpent in the garden of Eden that tempted Eve. However, many Singaporeans, irrespective of their religious upbringing, have an ingrained fear of snakes. This appears to be a universal trait which is well-illustrated in the following lines from a poem by D.H. Lawrence entitled *Snake*.

> *"The voices of my education said to me*
> *He must be killed,*
> *For in Sicily the black, black snakes are innocent, the gold are venomous.*
>
> *And voices in me said, If you were a man*
> *You would take a stick and break him now, and finish him off."*

Both Francis Lim and Dr Monty Lee are to be congratulated for having contributed sig-nificantly towards helping us dispel our fears in this book, as well as providing simple, but useful tips on what to do during snake encounters and how to treat snakebites. By creating a better understanding of our indigenous snake species, both Francis and Monty are help-ing to promote conservation in this region.

The magnificent spectacled Indian Cobra dramatises the
serpent worship found in the Hindu culture.

Francis has had a long association with reptiles and snakes in particular, and I know that this book is a labour of love. His expertise in this subject is well-demonstrated, and its publication will firmly place him amongst a select group of experts in this region. I am proud to work with Francis, and I know that I also speak for his colleagues at the Singapore Zoological Gardens. I also hope that the Zoo will continue to nurture such specialists in other fields of zoology in the future.

Executive Director
Singapore Zoological Gardens
4 July 1988

Preface

Snakes have generally been the least understood and most abused of all the animals. They are often regarded by many people as symbols of evil and danger. This is rather unfortunate because the majority of the 2 700 species of snakes found in the world today are basically harmless, in the sense that under normal circumstances, they seldom pose a significant danger to human lives.

Most snakes would prefer to avoid humans. When encountered, the snake's first reaction would be to try and escape. If it is cornered, it will then defend itself like any other wild animal — striking back and biting, if necessary. On the other hand, some snakes have learned to co-exist with us, usually to mutual advantage. The Common House Snake or Wolf Snake (*Lycodon aulicus*) is a good example as it adapts well to living in houses and buildings where its favourite prey, the house lizard, abounds. Rat snakes living close to human settlements feed on rats and mice which are considered pests by man.

Of the 139 species recorded in the region of Singapore and Peninsular Malaysia, only about 28% are venomous and therefore pose a danger to us. Among these venomous snakes are the cobras, kraits, coral snakes, vipers and sea snakes. It is therefore important that one is able to identify these venomous snakes and know something about their characteristics, and the nature of their habitats for the simple reason that there are records of people being fatally bitten by some of these snakes.

I have tried to be as comprehensive as possible, describing as many families, species and sub-species of snakes as can be found in this region. This attempt is not completely fulfilled as many snakes are rather secretive and some are rather rare, and so the opportunity to photograph them has yet to come. This modest book covers only about 75 species out of all the varieties of fascinating snake fauna existing in Southeast Asia, particularly those found in Singapore and Peninsular Malaysia. To identify snakes by scale counts and other technical descriptions of scale arrangements or dentition can be quite confusing to the general reader. This book, therefore emphasises the general body characteristics and colour, as well as the type of natural habitat as a reliable means of identification for each species. It must be noted, however, that body colouration may vary more or less according to the age, physical condition as well as geographical distribution of the snake. I have also taken the liberty to coin common names for some of the snakes when these are lacking in the standard published text for the benefit of the layman.

The chapter, **Snakes and Snakebites**, where my co-author Dr Monty Lee, has condensed some practical tips from firsthand material, may prove useful for outdoor enthusiasts and medical practitioners. For the reader who is keen to know how to deal with a trespassing snake, he will find the information in the chapter, **Snake Encounters**, useful.

It is our intention to promote a better understanding and appreciation of these fascinating snakes through this book. The natural history of many species is still not fully studied and understood. We lament the wanton destruction of many harmless snakes by ill-informed people who over-react as a consequence of their fear of snakes. As with all living things, snakes do have a part to play in maintaining the balance of nature. They share the world with us and rightly deserve a chance to live. We hope that this book will also serve as a valuable guide for all biology teachers and students as well as those keenly interested in some of the snakes found more commonly in this region.

Francis L.K. Lim
Dr Monty Lee Tat-Mong

Acknowledgements

The authors wish to express their sincere thanks to the following people who have provided them with the much-needed encouragement, support and assistance in the production of this book:

- Dr Ong Swee Law, Executive Chairman of the Singapore Zoological Gardens, for reading the manuscript and contributing his foreword;
- Mr Bernard Harrison, Executive Director of the Zoo, for his encouragement and foreword;
- Dr Lim Boo Liat for reading the text and his helpful suggestions;
- Dr S. K. Teo for his comments on the chapter on **Snakes and Snakebites**;
- A. F. Stimson and Colin McCarthy of the British Museum of Natural History for their assistance in identifying some snakes;
- Dr Stephen Ambu of the Institute for Medical Research, Malaysia, for his assistance in providing a study of snakebites in Peninsular Malaysia with special reference to Perlis Indera Kayangan and Kedah Darul Aman from 1979–1983;
- Ms Ilsa Sharp for editing and commenting on the original manuscript as well as giving her unwavering support over the years which eventually saw the book through;
- the kind and supportive colleagues of the Zoological, Public Relations and Education departments;
- our many helpful friends, in particular, Dr Leo Tan, Glenn, Alfie, Marshall, just to name a few.

Photo credits

Anthony Bogadek (*Psammodynastes pulverulentus*) p 75, Detlef Busse (Indian Snake Charmer and Cobra) p 6, Dr Lim Boo Liat (*Enhydrina schistosa*) p 96, Robin Stewart (*Lycodon effraenis*) p 55, Ken Rubeli (*Elaphe taeniura*) p 40.

Illustrations by Kelvin K.P. Lim. All other photographs used in the book are by Francis Lim.

List Of Photographs Used In The Descriptions Of Snakes

Pythons And Other Primitive Snakes

 1 Reticulated Python — contented after a meal 26
 2 Reticulated Python — female incubating eggs 27
 3 Blood Python 27
 4 Rock Python — adult 28
 5 Rock Python — baby 29
 6 Vestiges of the hind limbs, called "claws" or "spurs" 29
 7 Common Blind Snake 30
 8 Diard's Blind Snake 31
 9 Red-tailed Pipe Snake — with tail raised 32
10 Red-tailed Pipe Snake — juveniles with distinctly patterned ventrals 32
11 Iridescent Earth Snake — female with eggs 33
12 Iridescent Earth Snake — head 33
13 Elephant's Trunk Snake 34
14 File Snake 35

Non-venomous Colubrine Snakes

15 Keeled Slug Snake 37
16 Common Racer — adult 38
17 Common Racer — young in striking attitude 38
18 Copperhead Racer 39
19 Striped Racer 40-41
20 Red-tailed Racer 40-41
21 Keeled Rat Snake 42
22 Indo-Chinese Rat Snake — adult 43
23 Indo-Chinese Rat Snake — hatchling 43
24 Banded Rat Snake 44
25 Malayan Brown Snake 45
26 Striped Kukri Snake 46
27 Brown Kukri Snake — adult 46
28 Brown Kukri Snake — juvenile 47
29 Variable Reed Snake 48
30 Pink-headed Reed Snake 49
31 Dwarf Reed Snake 50
32 Orange-bellied Snake — variable form 51

33 Orange-bellied Snake — normal form   51
34 Painted Bronzeback   52
35 Elegant Bronzeback   53
36 Striped Bronzeback   53
37 Common House Snake or Wolf Snake   54
38 Scarce Wolf Snake   55
39 Indo-Chinese Wolf Snake   56
40 Black-headed Collared Snake   57
41 Chequered Keelback — adult swallowing a fish   58
42 Chequered Keelback — large clutch of eggs   58
43 Striped Keelback — head markings   59
44 Striped Keelback — specimen collected in Singapore   59
45 Red-necked Keelback — adult   60
46 Blue-necked Keelback   61
47 Red-necked Keelback — juvenile   61

Back-fanged Mildly Venomous Snakes

48 Paradise Tree Snake — adult with vertebral red spots   63
49 Paradise Tree Snake — adult without vertebral red spots   63
50 Golden Tree Snake — eggs hatching   64
51 Golden Tree Snake — adult   64
52 Twin-barred Tree Snake   65
53 Oriental Whip Snake — struggling with an agamid   66
54 Oriental Whip Snake — mainly tree-bound   67
55 Long-nosed Whip Snake   68-69
56 Keel-bellied Whip Snake   69
57 Puff-faced Water Snake — adult   70
58 Puff-faced Water Snake — baby   70
59 Dog-faced Water Snake   71
60 Bocourt's Water Snake   72
61 Plumbeous Water Snake   73
62 Rainbow Water Snake   73
63 Tentacled Snake   74-75
64 Tentacled Snake — head   74-75
65 Mock Viper   75
66 Mangrove Snake — in striking attitude   76
67 White-spotted Cat Snake   77
68 Dog-toothed Cat Snake   78
69 Jasper Cat Snake — full-length   79

70 Jasper Cat Snake — head   79
71 Green Cat-eyed Snake — in striking attitude   80
72 Green Cat-eyed Snake — long and slender green body   81

Front-fanged Venomous Snakes

73 Blue Coral Snake   83
74 Banded Coral Snake   84
75 Banded Krait   85
76 Malayan Krait   86
77 Red-headed Krait   87
78 Black Spitting Cobra — with hood outspread   88
79 Black Spitting Cobra — another form   89
80 Monocled Cobra   89
81 Common Chinese Cobra — full-length   90
82 Common Chinese Cobra — head   90
83 Philippine Cobra — back of hood with no markings   91
84 Philippine Cobra — full length   91
85 King Cobra/Hamadryad — baby   92
86 King Cobra/Hamadryad — adult   93
87 Amphibious Sea Snake   94
88 Amphibious Sea Snake — head and tail markings   95
89 Common Sea Snake   96
90 Hardwicke's Sea Snake   96-97
91 Banded Sea Snake   97
92 Eyelash Sea Snake — head   98
93 Eyelash Sea Snake — full-length   98
94 Olive Sea Snake   99
95 Malayan Pit Viper — female with eggs   101
96 Malayan Pit Viper — eggs hatching   101
97 Wagler's Pit Viper — juvenile   102
98 Wagler's Pit Viper — adult   102
99 Sumatran Pit Viper — full-length   103
100 Sumatran Pit Viper — fangs   103
101 Popes' Pit Viper — commonly occurs in montane forests   104
102 Popes' Pit Viper — capable of inflicting painful bites   105
103 Shore Pit Viper — form from Singapore   106
104 Shore Pit Viper — juvenile   107
105 Shore Pit Viper — form from Peninsular Malaysia/ Thailand   107

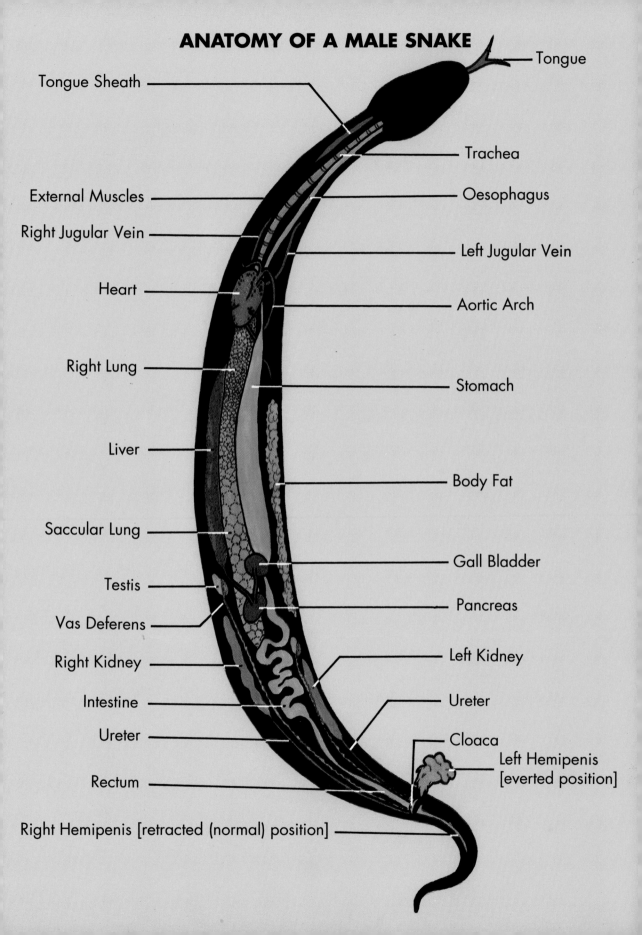

ANATOMY OF A MALE SNAKE

Tongue

Tongue Sheath

Trachea

External Muscles

Oesophagus

Right Jugular Vein

Left Jugular Vein

Heart

Aortic Arch

Right Lung

Stomach

Liver

Body Fat

Saccular Lung

Gall Bladder

Testis

Pancreas

Vas Deferens

Right Kidney

Left Kidney

Intestine

Ureter

Ureter

Cloaca

Rectum

Left Hemipenis
[everted position]

Right Hemipenis [retracted (normal) position]

Introduction

Southeast Asia certainly harbours one of the richest and most fascinating snake fauna in the world. The Malaysian region, including Sabah and Sarawak, has a combined total of 192 species of snakes which are found in all manner of habitats. Despite this immense serpentine variety, there is a remarkable dearth of knowledge of the biology of many of the snake species.

One reason could be that snakes are very difficult animals to study in the wild. They apparently do not have a set pattern of activity or territorial requirements as of the higher animals, like birds and primates. Chances are that snakes which have been disturbed in a particular area will not return to that place. Hence, people who encounter a snake in their premises rarely see the same snake again.

A large number of interesting facts, however, have been gathered through observations of captive snakes. It is possible, through experimentation, to discover the food preferences of captive specimens. Newly caught snakes are often sacrificed so that their stomach contents can be collected and analysed to help researchers determine the feeding habits of wild snakes. The data gathered will help herpetologists and reptile keepers keep snakes in captivity successfully since the provision of good, suitable food is one of the prerequisites. It can be argued that snakes in captivity are being fed well and in greater quantity than they would be in the wild. It seems that longevity records are normally achieved by contented serpents living under controlled, but ideal captive conditions. For example, the Anaconda (*Eunectes murinus*) of the jungles of South America has been recorded to live for about 31 years in captivity; the Boa Constrictor (*Constrictor constrictor*) of Central and South America came close to 27 years while most smaller species of snakes live up to 10 years or more.

Some snakes do breed readily in captivity; the clutch size of eggs, incubation period and subsequent growth of the young snakes are then studied in detail by herpetologists. On the other hand, most species have not yet bred under captive conditions, even when their requirements are apparently met in all respects. These are the snakes that make the job of their keepers more challenging and rewarding when captive breeding is finally induced.

Reptile medicine is a field where advances are continually being made in the isolation of reptilian diseases and the search for cures. Few people are aware that snakes do suffer from tuberculosis, enteritis, pneumonia and parasitic worms besides a host of captivity-associated ailments, like mouth-rot and amoebic dysentry. The medical management of captive reptiles is therefore of special interest to reptile keepers in zoos, personnel of herpetological institutions and reptile enthusiasts.

Snake-keeping as a hobby has not really caught on in this part of the world, unlike in some countries in Europe and the Americas, where snake clubs exist to cater to the needs of reptile hobbyists. Boa Constrictors and Rock Pythons (*Python molurus*) are among the favourites of reptile hobbyists. Not all snakes can be kept as pets or showpieces. Many of the small snakes mentioned in this book, for example the blind snakes and reed snakes are rather shy and secretive, as well as being special feeders, and are therefore not worth displaying in one's home. Similarly, venomous snakes should not be kept in the home, though they would make interesting conversation pieces! Such snakes should be kept only in zoos or by experts.

Francis L.K. Lim knows a handful of people who are crazy about snakes and keep a few at home as pets. The main reason for their taking up such an unusual hobby is that they regard snakes as not only fascinating, but also clean

Young children have little instinctive fear of snakes.

and delightful pets. Generally speaking, reptiles do not require constant care and attention. Hence, if you possess a pet whip snake and are intent on going on a vacation for a week or so, all you need to do is to ensure that there is sufficient drinking water, put in a few live geckos and the snake will take care of itself until you return. There is, however, one precaution. Tanks used for keeping snakes should be escape-proof. Other suitable snakes that can be kept as pets are baby Reticulated Pythons, grass snakes and kukri snakes. Feeding the snakes may take a little effort, as baby pythons eat mice, small birds and chicks; grass snakes do well on frogs and fishes, and kukri snakes relish egg yolks.

The sleek, green whip snake makes a suitable pet and its favourite food, the house lizard, can be easily caught in this region. Small whip snakes can be fed on houseflies and small frogs. It is good management to provide some branches for these arboreal snakes to climb and rest on.

Rock Pythons, when tamed at an early age, make excellent pets. They grow rapidly when fed regularly on mice, rats and birds. Larger pythons not only require larger food items, like whole chickens and rabbits, but also a more spacious place to live in. Do not handle snakes before and immediately after they have been fed. Always wash your hands after handling food for snakes. Unwashed hands may tempt a hungry pet to bite, as it relies largely on its tongue to identify food. Feeding times should be regular; small snakes are usually fed twice a week while larger snakes are fed once in a week or a fortnight. Though snakes are capable of fasting for long periods, regular feeding helps to maintain them in good health. Francis L.K. Lim would like to stress that it is cruel to attempt to keep any animal without first possessing some basic knowledge of its biology and needs. So, do find out all you can before taking up snake-keeping. And this book would not have been in vain if it helps people to make friends with snakes.

Snakes in Religions and Folklore

"…in my name they will cast out demons;

they will speak in new tongues;

they will pick up serpents, and if they drink any deadly thing, it will not hurt them; they will lay their hands on the sick, and they will recover."

— Mark 16: 17 – 18

The snake has had an unfavourable association with man ever since its biblical creation. In the Christian religion, the serpent nearly always becomes associated with the devil or something evil and hence, it is loathsome. Its unpopularity is the consequence of its masterminding man's fall into sin, suffering and death through subterfuge. Everybody knows of the story of Adam and Eve. God loves man so much that He sent His only son, Jesus, to redeem mankind so that we will become God's own again and regain the right to share in the glory of heaven thereafter. The devil, in his attempt to foil God's plan, tempted Jesus for 40 days in the desert soon after Jesus' baptism. And the snake crawling on its belly was a manifestation of the devil.

However, the snake does not always have a coloured place in the Bible. In the Book of Numbers (21: 4 – 9), God punishes the Israelites for their impatience and rebellion by sending poisonous snakes to the people. Many were bitten and killed. The repentant Israelites then asked Moses to pray to God to take the snakes away. The Lord replied and told Moses to make a bronze snake and put it on a pole in the desert so that anyone who was bitten could look at it and be healed.

In fact, the snake plays an important part in the religious services of a small fundamental Christian sect in the south-eastern parts of the United States of America. Followers of this sect hold dearly the Word of God as spoken in the gospel according to Mark 16: 17 – 18. It says "And these signs will accompany those who believe: in my name…they will pick

4

up serpents,..." Followers of the sect, having complete trust in God, not only openly handle deadly venomous snakes, like cobras and rattlesnakes with their bare hands, but also drink strychnine or other lethal concoctions so "as to confirm the Word of God". Though fatal accidents occasionally occur to the snake handlers, the participants continue to pray, sing and preach the gospel as they believe it should be spread.

The snake has also, at various times and places, played various roles in the religious beliefs and social organisations of many people in different lands. In Egypt, the cobra is venerated as the goddess Ejo and is not only worshipped by the Egyptians, but also featured prominently in the headdress of the ruler at that time. The Indians of Arizona and the aborigines of Australia both regard snakes or snake gods as bringers of rain to their land, with the former even performing a snake dance for this specific need. Many rites of some African tribes include a snake dance to ensure the fertility of a young woman.

In India, the deadly cobra is venerated as a divine creature and has been worshipped by devotees for thousands of years. Special occasions are celebrated, for example, the festival of Nagpanchmi which falls on the fifth day of the Hindu month of Shravana. During the festivities, processions of snake effigies are carried out and the devotees gather in temples to offer milk to images of snake gods. It is said in Hindu mythology that the Indian Cobra is regarded as a symbol of good fortune and fertility. Married women devotees who are childless are especially dedicated to the snake god whom they believe can bring them the joy of motherhood.

In Buddhist mythology, legend has it that the cobra, upon seeing the Lord Buddha meditating in the open, slithered up close to him and rose over his head. The cobra then spread its hood over him so as to protect him from the elements. When the Lord Buddha had finished with his meditation, he saw what the cobra had done, and in appreciation, blessed the snake by placing his index and middle fingers on its hood, thereby leaving an indelible pair of marks or 'eyes'.

Chinese folklore is rich in fables and legends which immortalise the snake. For example, there is a play entitled, "Madam White Snake", which is often enacted on stage.

The fable revolves round the spirit of the white snake which transformed itself into a beautiful lady who then fell in love with a scholar. The couple got married and had a son. This love story would have ended happily had it not been for the Jade Emperor's intervention. He was indignant over the couple's unnatural wedlock. The white snake's refusal to revert to its previous form resulted in a great battle in which the snake subsequently lost to the Jade Emperor in Heaven. Could it then be a coincidence that some people are rather reluctant to kill large, aged serpents because they believe that spirits reside in the snakes' bodies?

There is a local tale that warns one of killing a snake lest its mate should come slithering around, looking for revenge when one is off guard. This tale could have come about from a situation where a snake was recently killed and another one was suddenly spotted nearby, apparently seeking to take revenge.

Snakes are often revered together with other deities in some small Chinese temples, both here in Singapore and in Peninsular Malaysia. Huge snakes, usually pythons, are often kept in cages in the grounds of the temples and are worshipped by devotees who regard the serpents as symbols of good luck and prosperity. In Penang's famed Snake Temple, the deity, Chor Su Kong, stands among heaps of poisonous snakes which are all within touching distance. These snakes are usually Wagler's Pit Vipers. Worshippers come by the thousands for the annual celebrations of the deity's birthday, which falls on the sixth day of the Chinese first moon (Lunar calendar). They bring along with them offerings, like eggs, for the vipers. The presence of many sluggish vipers draping over the altars and branches has aroused the curiosity of people, especially tourists, over the years.

The most remarkable snake-man relationship has been that between the snake and the snake charmer.

The most remarkable snake-man relationship has been that between the snake and the snake charmer. Though some snake charmers mutilate their snakes so as to render them harmless, most professional charmers treat theirs with respect and dignity, and would consider it unthinkable to subject their snakes to such cruel treatment. Snake charmers are adept at catching and handling snakes, an art which they ultimately manifest by convincing the audience of their ability to "charm" the deadly cobra so that it "dances" to the melody flowing from the charmer's flute. And they usually succeed, for few among their captive audience are aware of the fact that cobras, like all snakes, are deaf to airborne sounds and therefore cannot hear the music. Instead, they dance to the rhythmical movements of the charmer's hands and flute.

In the other extreme, snakes are often greatly exploited by man to satisfy his whims and fancies. Some people believe that the gall bladder of a snake, when taken with rice wine, is a seeming cure for rheumatism and hypertension. Chinese folk medicine promotes the drinking of snake soup as a cure for various skin ailments; and in Hong Kong, the soup is taken to keep the body warm in winter. In Taiwan, concoctions like the snake cocktail, a heady mixture of snake blood and brandy, are often gulped down with relish. Whole snake is also dunked in wine, and the contents, after some ageing, are said to be an antidote for snakebites as well as a general tonic for the body when consumed. Such purported cures and tonics have yet to be proven, but these beliefs have resulted in the slaughter of hundreds of thousands of snakes annually in the Asian region.

To continue listing the roles that snakes play in religious beliefs, cultures and folklore would be beyond the scope of this book. All in all, snake-man relationships have been colourful, imaginary, emotional and even controversial, and will continue to be so for a long time to come.

Snake Encounters

The majority of the 139 species of land and sea snakes found in the region of Singapore and Peninsular Malaysia belong to the non-venomous and the mildly venomous groups. The latter actually comprises the nocturnal cat snakes, as well as a number of species of tree and water snakes, which possess rear fangs and venom glands which are located at the back of the upper jaws. Their venom is rather weak and is therefore generally regarded as incapable of causing fatalities.

The really dangerous snakes inhabiting this area are the three species of nocturnal kraits, four species of coral snakes, two species of highly irritable cobras, eight species of vipers and about twenty-two species of sea snakes. Deaths have resulted from bites by some of these snakes, but fortunately, such incidents are rather rare.

The majority of vipers inhabiting this region belong to the pit viper group — they possess heat-sensitive pits along the upper lips. These pits serve as a means of detecting the body warmth of warm-blooded prey like rats at night. Bites from the terrestrial Malayan Pit Vipers have been a common occurrence in the northern states of Peninsular Malaysia, where the local folk usually walk around barefooted. Viper-bite victims normally experience severe pain, intense swelling of the bitten limb, bleeding from the wounds and nausea. Death from local viper bites is fortunately uncommon.

How To Catch A Snake

What should one do when one encounters a snake on one's premises? Or say, in the field? The first thing one should NOT do is panic! Chances are that the cause of your excitement and anxiety is more often than not a non-venomous and rather harmless snake. Below is a general introduction to some common groups of snakes and the methods of disposing them.

Pythons

There are only 2 species of pythons inhabiting Singapore and Peninsular Malaysia, and one can hardly mistake them for venomous snakes owing to their large size. Pythons are commonly found in jungles near water, but may invade moderately populated or even densely built-up areas. Large pythons are dangerous because of their constrictive power and vicious bite. Striking pythons will bite and pull back, inflicting deep gashes on the victim and causing severe bleeding. Two or more persons are needed to overpower a large python. It can be rendered helpless once its head is securely gripped with the hands. Smaller pythons can be easily restrained using snake hooks or sticks.

Rat Snakes, Racers, Paradise Tree Snakes /Bronzebacks and Common House Snakes

These fast-moving snakes are active during the day. They are absolute masters in their element and are hard to catch. They occasionally enter gardens and homes in search of rats and lizards, and should be left alone since they do not stay long. Do not corner them unless you want them for specimens as they will bite. However, they are not venomous. The Common House Snakes possess the uncanny ability to invade high-rise buildings, for specimens have been caught high above ground level. Always wear leather gloves if you have to handle these wild snakes.

Leather gloves afford effective protection from bites by a small snake like this Golden Tree Snake.

Blind Snakes, Earth Snakes, Pipe Snakes and Kukris

These snakes are generally timid, secretive and mainly nocturnal . They commonly occur in loose, cultivated earth, as well as in clumps of grass, where they feed on insects, lizards, amphibians and mice. One should leave them alone as they are harmless.

Whip Snakes

These green, slender-bodied snakes have spear-shaped heads that make them look deadly. They usually remain motionless, but have the disturbing habit of darting forward suddenly towards one's face. When tamed, the whip snake makes a good pet.

Vipers

They are easily recognised by their arrow-shaped heads and stout bodies which make them look sluggish and inactive. The Malayan Pit Viper and the Shore Pit Viper can be rather nasty when provoked. Baby vipers are usually encountered as they often move about in search of food and shelter. One can easily pick them up with the end of a long stick and deposit them back into the bushes out of harm's way. If one is intent on killing the snakes, then the *coup de grace* can be applied by breaking the snakes' backs with a sharp blow from a stick.

Cobras

There are two types — the Indian Cobra or the Black Spitting Cobra and the King Cobra. Black Spitting Cobras are active at night when they hunt for amphibians and rodents, occasionally entering gardens when prowling. A well-lit garden deters such snakes from visiting. Care should be taken when confronting the Black Spitting Cobra, for a well-aimed 'spit' of venom in the eyes can have painful consequences. The King Cobra is deadly because of its size and the large quantity of venom it can secrete. Fortunately, it is rare and occurs in scrub country and forests. Do not disturb a pile of vegetable debris in the field as it could be the nest of the King Cobra — a brooding female is said to be aggressive when guarding her eggs. All cobras should be left alone when encountered in the field.

Figure A

Figure B

There are no fixed guidelines when catching animals, whether tame or wild. Many factors have to be taken into consideration when catching a wild snake — the circumstances and type of snake, as well as facilities available at hand. Therefore, the methods described below are, at best, only very general. The use of equipment is dictated by the kind of snake in relation to the type of environment in which it is to be captured.

The most commonly used tool for restraining snakes is the snake hook or a simple forked stick. Snake hooks are made of metal, usually aluminium alloy because of its light weight, and are specially designed for use in zoos. They have a hook on one end, a long shaft and a handle on the other (Fig. A and Fig. B). The bigger the snake that is to be restrained, the longer the snake hook that will have to be used. In the absence of a snake hook, a forked branch (Fig. C) will do just fine.

When catching a snake using a hook, the snake is usually lifted up by the hook and placed onto an open space. This allows one room to move about should the snake strike back. Small snakes can be easily lifted up by the hook and dropped into the open mouth of cloth bags or bottles. For larger snakes, the hook is used to press down onto the neck (Fig. D and Fig. E). Be careful not to choke the snake. The pressure applied should be reasonably sufficient to prevent the snake from breaking loose.

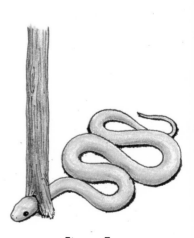

Figure C   Figure D   Figure E

11

Figure F

Once the snake has been secured, the free hand must move quickly to a position just behind the hook to obtain a good grip on the neck of the snake (Fig.F). The hook can then be lifted off. This method of restraining is very effective for snakes up to 2.5 metres long. Snakes that are larger, stronger and longer than this length are best restrained using the snare (loop and handle).

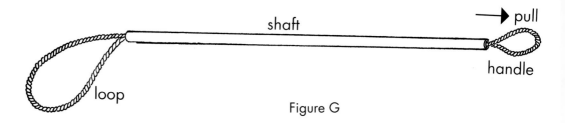

Figure G

shaft

pull

handle

loop

The snare (Fig. G) is recommended for use in restraining large snakes, like pythons and large cobras. Owing to the size and strength of these snakes, 2 or more persons are required to restrain the snake, and teamwork is important. Let's say, for example, there is a big python coiled up on a branch in a tree and it refuses to budge even when prodded with a stick. The first step to take, when using the snare, is to manoeuvre the loop around the snake's neck and secure it by pulling the handle. Then attempt to pull the snake down. However, sometimes it stubbornly decides to stay put and so the second catcher goes into action (unless you are bent on pulling the head off the snake!). By a combination of pulling and prodding, the snake would be persuaded to release its coils eventually and slide down onto the ground where it can be pinned down with a hook and then bundled into a gunnysack (Fig. H).

Figure H

The gunnysack must be securely tied at the opening since snakes are wonderful escape artists. The authors recommend that the captured snake be transferred to a nature reserve and released there. Most people prefer to send the captured snakes to the local zoo, usually with a sense of relief.

Snakes and Snakebites

Out of 139 species of land and sea snakes known to occur in the region of Singapore and Malaysia, only 39 species are considered venomous, and they include a group of 22 species of sea snakes which we do not frequently encounter. Yet the very thought of needle-sharp snake fangs embedded in one's flesh and oozing venom is enough to send shivers down the spines of most people. (Indeed, some people have been known to succumb through sheer fright upon mere encounters with snakes which did not even bite them!)

The really dangerous snakes are the unpredictable co-bras and kraits. Mishaps with coral snakes are rare, but have been documented. Coral snakes are potentially dangerous as there is no readily available antivenin for treatment of bites inflicted by them. Hence, these beautiful snakes should be treated with due respect when encountered in the field. Bites by vipers are well-documented in many Malaysian states. It was reported by Lim (1980) that the Malayan Pit Viper was responsible for about 55.8% of the 227 snakebite cases admitted to the Alor Setar General Hospital in the state of Kedah Darul Aman. In another study, (*Lim, 1982*), Dr Lim Boo Liat compiled an overall reported snakebite cases for all the 11 states of Peninsular Malaysia from 1960 – 1970. During that period, there were altogether 53 216 bites inflicted by both venomous and non-venomous snakes, which resulted in a mortality rate of 0.47% or 249 deaths.

In spite of all these frightening data, it must be noted that snakes are not overly aggressive, and basically, they kill in order to obtain food to survive. Hence, most of the snakebite cases reported have been victims who had accidentally or intentionally provoked the otherwise peaceable serpent. Consequently, the location of most bites is at the extremities of the body such as the feet, hands or fingers. A review by S.K. Teo in 1982 on snakebites treated at the Changi Hospital, Singapore, revealed that 81% of 27 snakebite incidents occurred in the region of the toe, foot/ankle, thumb/finger or hand. Snakebites in Singapore are, however, very uncommon. An estimated 40 cases of bites are treated at the hospitals and clinics every year. The mortality rate is even more insignificant, there being only one death (from a suspected Blue Coral snakebite) in the past three years.

In a study of snakebites in Peninsular Malaysia from 1979 – 1983 by Stephen Ambu and Lim Boo Liat (1988), it was revealed that the range of bites per year was between 5 077 and 5 492. They also found that the 11 – 30 age group (victims) had the highest number of snakebites. The northern states of Perlis Indera Kayangan and Kedah Darul Aman had the highest number of snakebite incidents, i.e. about 50% of the mean total of 5 347 snakebites during the five-year survey period.

The formidable fangs of this pit viper are over 10 mm long.

The following table lists the total number of snakebite cases reported in the study for all the 11 states of Peninsular Malaysia from 1979 – 1983.

Total number of snakebites in Peninsular Malaysia 1979 – 1983 (Ambu & Lim, 1988)

Year \\ State	1979	1980	1981	1982	1983	Population	Mean no. bites / year / 1 000 population
Perlis Indera Kayangan	410	379	385	414	339	148 300	385 (2.60)
Kedah Darul Aman	211	2 070	2 100	2 103	2 144	1 116 100	2 105 (1.80)
Perak Darul Ridzuan	556	527	604	594	579	1 805 200	572 (0.32)
Selangor Darul Ehsan	225	239	282	293	189	1 515 500	251.6 (0.17)
N.Sembilan Darul Khusus	163	167	155	174	169	573 600	165.6 (0.29)
Malacca	82	56	44	72	64	464 800	63.6 (0.14)
Johor Darul Takzim	150	161	205	188	206	1 638 200	182 (0.11)
Pahang Darul Makmur	574	384	385	325	330	798 800	399.6 (0.50)
Terengganu Darul Iman	241	168	261	264	257	540 600	238.2 (0.44)
Kelantan Darul Naim	304	341	385	315	359	893 800	340.8 (0.38)
Penang	195	188	318	336	229	954 600	253.2 (0.27)
Total	5 451	5 077	5 509	5 492	5 204	10 449 500	5 347 (0.50)

Our purpose is not to say that all snakes are friendly or completely harmless animals. Admittedly, some are a potential danger to human life. However, snakebites are not at all common. THE BEST ANTIDOTE IS DON'T GET BITTEN. But should one be unfortunate enough to be bitten after all, then the next best thing is TO KNOW WHAT TO DO.

Some Tips On The Prevention Of Snakebites

Around The Premises:

1 Trim grass well, and prune dense foliage and undergrowth regularly.

2 Remove unwanted timber and pots as these are favourite hiding places for snakes.

3 Keep branches and creepers clear of windows. Snakes may use them to get into houses.

4 Fill all burrows, holes and crevices in walls and the ground. They provide excellent hiding places for snakes.

5 Screen all ventilation openings and sewerage outlets with weather-resistant mesh or gratings.

6 Dispose of uneaten food properly, otherwise this may attract rats which in turn invite their predators, the snakes.

7 If an area is infested with rats, get a pest control company to exterminate them.

8 Insects, amphibians and lizards may attract their predators, the tree snakes. It is advisable to fumigate your premises periodically if you are living in the countryside.

9 Rearing of chickens, pigeons and other small animals, like guinea pigs, may attract snakes.

10 Drain ponds regularly and keep them clean. The Reticulated Python is especially fond of water. Improperly kept ponds tend to harbour frogs and toads which are preyed upon by many species of snakes.

Out In The Field:

1 Keep your eyes open in snake-infested areas, and look where you are stepping or sitting.

2 Wear protective leather or rubber boots or shoes.

3 Wear baggy trousers of reasonably thick material.

4   Avoid tall grass, thick bushes and rocky places over-grown with weeds.

5   Avoid walking in the dark when out in the field because many snakes are active at night. Use a torch if you have to do so.

6   Be careful when you sleep on the ground . Your body warmth may attract a pit viper or a coral snake!

7   Never step out at night barefooted, or without a torch.

8   Don't stick your hand or foot into any holes in rocks, trees or the ground — there may be snakes in these.

9   On encountering a snake, DON'T RUN. It is safer to keep perfectly still or back away slowly. The snake just needs room to move off, and will do so in most circumstances.

10 Do not molest any snake. Provocation may lead to a snake biting.

11 Do not tease others with a dead snake . It might not be dead enough!

12 Freshly killed snakes collected for identification purposes must be carefully handled using a stick, or with gloves.

What To Do When Bitten By A Snake

1   Remain calm. Two out of 3 victims are injected with very little or no venom. In the latter case, no specific treatment is required. Venomous snakes use their venom to kill their prey. They bite in defence, and usually do not inject their venom.

2   Identify the snake. This is very important if the doctors are to give the right antidote. Injecting the wrong type of antivenin is not only useless, but may also endanger the victim's life.

3 Apply first aid immediately and arrange for hospitalisation. Do not await the development of symptoms. If you are the victim and all alone, then walk slowly. Don't run for help.

4 The correct antivenin is the only treatment of proven value. Hospitals usually have stocks of antivenin, and doctors are capable of treating snakebites and cases of adverse serum reaction and shock.

5 Prompt medical treatment, reassurance and bedrest are the keys to a full recovery.

Immediate Treatment — First Aid

1 The victim is usually shocked and frightened; assurance and soothing are essential.

2 Inspect the bite:
Venomous snakebite — two clean puncture wounds — indicative of fang marks — swelling and discolouration when venom has been injected.

Non-venomous snakebite — semi-circular rows of punctures.

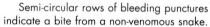
Semi-circular rows of bleeding punctures indicate a bite from a non-venomous snake.

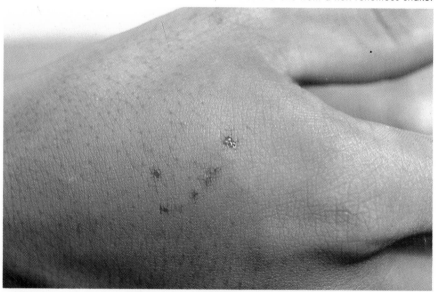

3   Immobilize the bitten area. This can delay absorption of venom.

4   Apply a firm but NOT tight tourniquet above the bite wound. Use a piece of cloth, a handkerchief or other material. Release for half a minute after every 10 – 15 minutes' grip.

5   Do NOT cut or squeeze the bite wound as this will only accelerate the spread of venom.

6   You may suck the wound and spit out, but first ensure that there are no cuts or ulcers in your mouth as the venom may enter into your system and affect you.

7   Apply an ice pack, if available, on the bite wound. This may delay the spread of venom.

8   Do not pour tobacco juice, kerosene, or cover the wound with unknown herbs, grass or mud.

9   Clean the wound and cover it with mild antiseptic lotion.

10   Do not offer any alcoholic drink as this may accelerate circulation of venom in the system.

11   You may give an analgesic (painkiller), but not morphine as it may aggravate the respiratory depression in poisoning by cobra venom.

12   If the victim's eyes have been spat at by the Black Spitting Cobra, do not rub the eyes. Wash them immediately with plain, preferably running water or better still, saline solution. If water is not available, human saliva or urine can be substituted. The victim's eyes usually become painful and swollen.

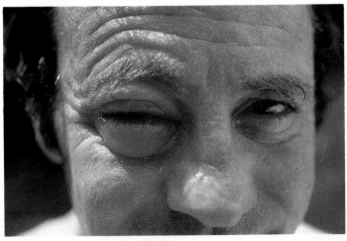

The victim's right eye is swollen one hour after being spat at by a Black Spitting Cobra.

13 Send the victim to the nearest hospital as soon as possible. Artificial respiration is to be given when there is weakness of the respiratory muscles.

14 Whenever possible, kill the offending snake, and take it with you for correct identification. If the snake has escaped or gone into hiding, do not search for it as you may end up getting bitten too.

In The Hospital

1 Identify the snake, if available, and determine whether it is venomous.

2 If there is no local swelling, most probably there has been no venom injected. In more than one-third of land snakebites, no venom has been injected. Thus, no antivenin is required, but the doctor may give Vitamin B Complex intramuscularly just to reassure the patient. The multiple teeth marks caused by a non-venomous snakebite should be cleaned with antiseptic lotion. The doctor may give an antitoxoid injection as a precaution.

3 If there is local swelling and/or dead skin, and the venom has not affected the rest of the body, no antivenin is recommended. You may give Paracetamol (an aspirin-like analgesic) to relieve burning pain. Release the tourniquet if applied; leave the bite wound alone (interference often exposes it to infection), and give antibiotics to prevent possible secondary infection.

4 Antivenin is the only reliable cure if a substantial amount of venom has been injected.

5 Specific antivenin — the one prepared for the particular species of snake responsible for the bite — is preferred to a polyvalent (multi-species) one.

6 It is not advisable to give antivenin unless serious symptoms are evident.

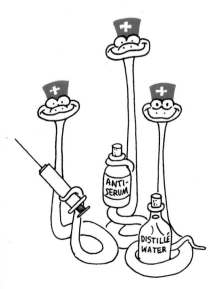

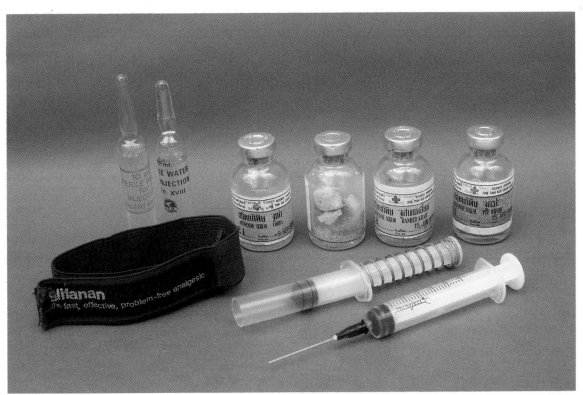

A tourniquet, specific antivenin, suction and injection syringes

7 Administer antivenin only in the presence of trained medical personnel and be prepared for anaphylactic shock (reaction to the injected material).

8 Test patient's sensitivity to antivenin by giving 0.2 ml subcutaneously first, and observe for 30 minutes.

9 If no adverse reaction occurs, administer the required amount of antivenin diluted in 200 ml of saline solution by slow intravenous drip; the whole volume in about an hour.

10 For a patient with a known allergic history, two intravenous drips should be set up: one containing antivenin, hydrocortisone and antihistamine, and the other containing adrenaline. If there is a reaction, the adrenaline can be given immediately.

11 For children, it is recommended that half to two thirds of a dose should be given.

12 If there is no improvement after the first dose of antivenin, a repeat treatment may be given an hour later.

Types Of Venom

There are basically 3 types of venom amongst venomous snakes found in the region.

The elapids, which include cobras, kraits and coral snakes, have neurotoxic venom, which attacks the nervous system. Victims eventually die of respiratory failure.

Sea snake venom is myotoxic and affects the muscles, causing aches and pains. Death is due to hyperkalemia and kidney failure resulting from destruction of muscular tissue.

Viper venom is both cytotoxic and haemotoxic: it damages the blood vessels, destroys blood cells, and in some cases, prevents blood clotting resulting in spontaneous and uncontrolled bleeding. Death is not common, but in the case of excessive blood loss, the victim's life may be in danger.

A quick reference to venomous snakebites is provided in the table below:

VENOMOUS SNAKE	VENOM TYPE	SYMPTOMS
Cobras Kraits Coral snakes	Neurotoxic	Little local pain and swelling, drowsiness, difficulty in speaking, swallowing, drooping upper eye-lid, stiff movement or paralysis
Sea snakes	Myotoxic	General muscular pain, slight paralysis and red-brown urine (myoglobinuria)
Vipers	Cytotoxic Haemotoxic	Intense pain, massive swelling and bleeding, dizziness, nausea, blood-stained spit or pinkish urine (haemoglobinuria)

Some Fantastic Facts About Snakes

Here are some questions which you may have asked yourself. You will find the answers to the questions not only concise and concrete but also enlightening.

How many species of snakes are there in the world?

Herpetologists (people who study reptiles) have given estimates of between 2 000 and 3 000.

Which is the longest snake in the world?

The Reticulated Python (*Python reticulatus*) is certainly the longest snake, with a recorded length of 9.5 m. The South American Anaconda (*Eunectes murinus*) has an estimated length of 12.5 m which is yet to be proven.

Which is the smallest snake in the world?

The Dwarf Blind Snake (*Leptotyphlops humilis*) found in the United States of America, and measuring only 10 cm long, is the world's smallest snake.

Is there any type of snake which can outrun a man?

No snake can actually outrun a man in a race; the many native stories about snakes moving at fantastic speeds are simply tales.

How many species of venomous snakes are there in the world?

Herpetologists have estimated that about 300 species, or roughly 11% of the 2 000 to 3 000 species of snakes, are venomous.

How do you distinguish between a venomous and a non-venomous snake?

Most non-venomous snakes have numerous, closely-set, small teeth while their venomous counterparts have, in addition, a pair or more of enlarged, specialised teeth for injecting venom, during a bite. These venom fangs may be hollow or grooved, and are located either in the front part or the back part of the upper jaw. Some venomous snakes are conspicuously colourful although they are nocturnal, for example, the coral snakes and kraits. The bright colours act as a warning that says "leave me alone, or else!" The cobras are easily recognised by their erect bodies and outspread hoods when disturbed. Vipers are generally stout-bodied and have arrow-shaped heads. Sea snakes are distinguished from the non-deadly freshwater snakes by their flattened tails.

Which is the most venomous snake in the world?

The Asiatic King Cobra or Hamadryad is generally considered by experts to be the most deadly by virtue if its size and the large quantity of venom it can secrete.

Do cobras give out poisonous gas when they hiss?

No. This belief is actually a misinterpretation of the fact that some cobras do spit venom with an accuracy of up to 2 m into the eyes of the victim, causing pain and eventual blindness if the eyes are not washed immediately.

Is the Oriental Whip Snake deadly, and can it disconnect its head to spear passersby?

The Oriental Whip Snake, known locally as *ching zhu se*, is back-fanged, but there are no records of any serious bites by this snake. Its uncanny habit of staring and suddenly darting forward towards the victim's head has earned it the notorious reputation of being able to detach its arrow-shaped head to impale the unfortunate victim. This of course is not true.

**Do snakes sting
with their tongues?**

The tongue of a snake is only a sensory organ. It is used in conjunction with the Jacobson's organs (pit-like sensory buds located in the roof of the mouth) to pick up scent and identify the smell, especially of potential prey.

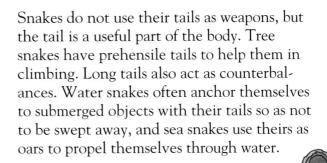

**Do snakes sting
with their tails?**

Snakes do not use their tails as weapons, but the tail is a useful part of the body. Tree snakes have prehensile tails to help them in climbing. Long tails also act as counterbalances. Water snakes often anchor themselves to submerged objects with their tails so as not to be swept away, and sea snakes use theirs as oars to propel themselves through water.

**Can snakes withstand
the extremes
of heat and cold?**

Being cold-blooded, snakes need to bask in the sun. Once their optimum temperature is reached, they move into the shade to cool off, or they will die of over-heating. Likewise, snakes will also die of extreme cold.

**Can snakes change
their body colours like
the chameleon?**

No, snakes cannot change their body colours at will. Some snakes may inflate their bodies so that hidden colours between their scales show out. This usually happens when they are disturbed.

What is moulting?

Moulting is the process of shedding old skin. In snakes, it is known as "sloughing", and begins when the snake rubs against rough objects. The snake then slowly peels and crawls out of its old skin, which is called a slough.

**How long can a
snake fast?**

Depending on the kind of snake, some can fast from a few weeks to several months. Large pythons have been recorded to fast for as long as a year.

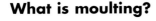

Pythons and Other Primitive Snakes

Family Boidae (Boas and Pythons)

Pythons are relatively large snakes that are active during dusk. They are often found coiled up in the trees. Their eyesight is well-developed, and vestiges of the hind limbs are present as claw-like structures on either side of the vent or cloaca. These snakes kill their prey by constriction. Only one genus occurs in Southeast Asia. There are two species of pythons occurring in the Singapore and Peninsular Malaysia region. Another species, the Rock Python, occurs in Thailand.

Genus Python

Reticulated Python
Python reticulatus   Non-venomous

The Reticulated Python is known to be the longest of all snakes, attaining a maximum length of between 10 and 15 m. Its normal prey consists of warm-blooded animals from chickens, pigs, goats and monkeys to small deer, which it can subdue. The prey is swallowed whole; the snake's jaws are not rigidly joined and thus can be stretched wide to accommodate bulky food items. This python is normally found in the jungle, especially close to water. It can also be found inhabiting rural and urban settlements. Small pythons can easily be

A Reticulated Python — contented after a meal of 2 guinea pigs

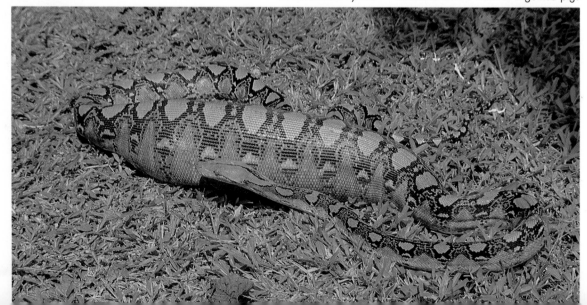

A female Reticulated Python incubating her clutch of eggs

captured and tamed, but adults are dangerous as they can deliver vicious bites, and their powerful coils may be too much for a man to handle. The female python lays from 20 to 50 eggs, rarely up to 100. The eggs adhere together in a mass, which the female coils around and incubates for a period of between 75 and 90 days. Baby pythons look similar to adults and measure about 60 cm in length.

Blood Python
Python curtus

Non-venomous

The Blood Python is also called the Short Python because of its rather short and stout body. Its head is small, and the upper lip of its mouth has two heat-sensitive pits instead of four on each side as in the Reticulated Python. These heat-sensory organs aid the snake in locating the presence of warm-blooded prey in the dark interiors of their jungle habitat. Small mammals, like rats and squirrels, as well as birds, are taken. About 10 to 15 eggs are laid, and are coiled and incubated by the female. It has been found that brooding pythons are capable of increasing their body temperature higher than the surrounding temperature. The young emerge in about 70 days and are about 40 cm long. Adult Blood Pythons reach a length of 3 m.

Rock Python
Python molurus bivittatus

Non-venomous

This beautiful python is distributed from Burma, Thailand to Southern China and Hong Kong. Its habitat ranges from jungles, scrub country to montane forests and areas close to water, for it can swim well. Its food consists of warm-blooded animals, like monkeys, small deer and pigs, which are seized in a lightning strike and then constricted till death by suffocation occurs.

Mating occurs in the early part of the year, after which about 9 to 54 eggs are laid and incubated by the female. Herpetologists, observing captive brooding pythons, found that when the surrounding air temperature drops, the snakes were able to raise and maintain the incubating temperature within the coils by quivering muscular contractions and heavy breathing. The eggs hatch in about $2\frac{1}{2}$ months. Baby Rock Pythons are brightly coloured and patterned. They are easily tamed and hence are popular with reptile enthusiasts and enlightened children. The Rock Python has been recorded to live for over 34 years in captivity, attaining a length of about 7 m.

Brightly-coloured baby
Rock Python

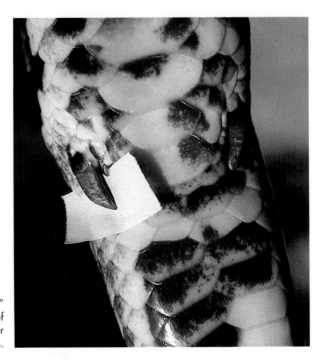

Vestiges of the hind limbs, called "claws"
or "spurs", are present on either side of
the cloaca. Male pythons have bigger
claws than females.

Family Typhlopidae (Blind Snakes)

Snakes belonging to this family are generally known as blind snakes. These are small, burrowing snakes with secretive habits. Their eyes are rudimentary and are covered by scales. Vestiges of the pelvic girdles may or may not be present. Two genera comprising 5 species are found in the Singapore and Peninsular Malaysia region. Of these, 2 species are described.

Genus Ramphotyphlops

Common Blind Snake   Non-venomous
Ramphotyphlops braminus

The Common Blind Snake is rather worm-like in appearance, and its short tail ends in a point which helps it anchor as it burrows into the soil. This snake is widely distributed, commonly inhabiting gardens or cultivated soil, as well as under stones or logs. It is nocturnal and feeds on soft-bodied insects. It reproduces by laying eggs, about 2 to 7 in number. An adult Blind Snake can reach up to 15 cm in length.

The Common Blind Snake is sometimes mistaken for a worm.

The short, blunt tail is used as an anchor when burrowing underground.

Genus Typhlops

Diard's Blind Snake
Typhlops diardi muelleri

Non-venomous

This blind snake has a very contrasting coloration, being dark above and light below. Its snout is very rounded, and its short tail ends in a spine. The belly scales are characteristically reduced, as in all blind snakes. It is nocturnal, appearing at dusk to hunt for other snakes and mollusks among the leaf litter. Its mouth is small and barely distensible. About 5 to 14 young are born in a litter. It is completely harmless and grows to about 30 to 48 cm long.

Family Aniliidae (Pipe Snakes)

These are rather stout-bodied snakes of primitive origin as they possess traces of the pelvic girdles. Their eyes are very small, and the tail is short and blunt. They spend most of the time hiding under leaves, or burrowing into loose earth. Two genera occur in Singapore and Peninsular Malaysia, each represented by a single species. Only *Cylindrophis* is described here.

The Red-tailed Pipe Snake with its tail raised

The underside of the juvenile Red-tailed Pipe Snake is distinctly patterned.

Genus Cylindrophis

Red-tailed Pipe Snake
Cylindrophis rufus   Non-venomous

The Red-tailed Pipe Snake is sometimes called the Two-headed Snake because of its habit of hiding its head under its coils and raising its short tail. It wriggles its tail about to confuse a would-be predator as to which is the real head. The underside of the tail is reddish in colour, and acts as a warning signal. It is, however, a mild-mannered snake that does not attempt to bite even when first handled. About 5 to 10 young are born in a litter. Adult snakes can reach about 90 cm in length. A 75-cm-long Red-tailed Pipe Snake captured by the staff of the Singapore Science Centre, gave birth to 5 young in mid-August; each young snake averaged 20.5 cm in length.

Family Xenopeltidae (Earth Snakes)

This unique family is represented by only one genus and one species, the distinction being due to the unusual and primitive features of the skull, and scale arrangements on the head.

Genus Xenopeltis

Iridescent Earth Snake
Xenopeltis unicolor

Non-venomous

This one-metre-long burrowing snake has a somewhat flattened head with a rounded snout and small eyes. It is commonly found in the lowlands, and lives in loose soil, clumps of grass and under logs. It is sometimes called the Sunbeam Snake due to the highly iridescence of the scales in sunlight. It is a gentle, nocturnal creature, and it feeds on amphibians, mice and other snakes. With regard to reproduction, it was observed that one 70-cm-long Iridescent Earth Snake laid a clutch of three white elongated eggs, which measured, on the average, 58 mm in length and 18 mm in diameter. The young Iridescent Earth Snakes have a white, collar-like band around the neck region.

Female with eggs

The Iridescent Earth Snake is well-adapted to a subterranean way of life.

The inoffensive Elephant's Trunk Snake is widely hunted for its skin.

Family Acrochordidae (Water Snakes)

These are sluggish, aquatic snakes. Their entire bodies are covered with uniform, granular scales which are rough to the touch. These water snakes give birth to live young that are capable of independent existence soon after birth. The diet of these snakes consists mainly of fish and eels. The family *Acrochordidae* is represented by 2 genera, with a single species each, and are found in the Singapore and Peninsular Malaysia region.

Genus Acrochordus

Elephant's Trunk Snake
Acrochordus javanicus

Non-venomous

It is a slow-moving and stout-bodied snake that can grow up to a length of 2 m or so. Being strictly aquatic, it is virtually helpless on land. The unusual baggy appearance gives rise to its similarly unusual name. It is commonly found in sluggish rivers, ditches and streams, and occurs in either fresh or brackish water where it feeds on fish and eels. Though normally inoffensive, it can and will bite if roughly handled.

It commonly burrows itself into river banks and under submerged tree roots where it remains in hiding until dusk when it appears to hunt for food. The Elephant's Trunk Snake is itself hunted for its skin which is processed into ornamental leather. The young are born in the water — a litter may number from 25 to 32, and the newborn snakes are about 46 cm in length.

Genus Chersydrus

File Snake
Chersydrus granulatus

Non-venomous

Like the Elephant's Trunk Snake, the entire body of this snake is also covered with numerous minute, granular scales. The belly scales are absent. Instead, there is a fold or pleat of skin along the mid-ventral line. The File Snake inhabits river mouths and mangrove swamps along the sea coast. Fish and eels form its normal diet. It is ovo-viviparous — the embryos develop inside the body. In late April, one File Snake was found to have 7 fully developed embryos, each averaging 23 cm long. The adult File Snake grows to a length of about 1 m.

The File Snake is distinctly marked and easily recognisable.

Non-venomous Colubrine Snakes

Family Colubridae

The Colubrine snakes make up the vast majority of Asiatic land snakes. Most of them have well-developed ventral scales and large, symmetrically arranged scales on the head. A few types have grooved poison fangs at the rear of the upper jaw, and as their venom is generally considered weak, they are believed to be incapable of inflicting fatal bites on healthy adult humans. The family *Colubridae* is divided into several sub-families. As a note on distribution, the word "region" used in this book refers to Singapore and Peninsular Malaysia.

Sub-family Pareinae (Slug Snakes)

There are about 5 species of these unique snakes distributed throughout this region. The main characteristic of this sub-family lies in the arrangement of the chin-shields, which are separated by a suture instead of a normal median groove, that is, a straight groove along the middle of the underside of the lower jaw. The mouths of these snakes are therefore only slightly distensible, and they feed largely on snails and slugs. The head is large with a short and blunt snout. Only 1 species is described here.

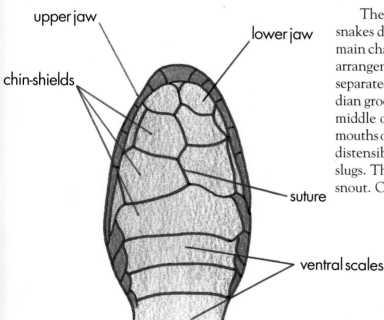

upper jaw

lower jaw

chin-shields

suture

ventral scales

Chin-shield arrangements of a Slug Snake

The Keeled Slug Snake inhabits damp, well-watered places where its prey abounds.

Genus Pareas

Keeled Slug Snake
Pareas carinatus

Non-venomous

The brown head of this snake has two black streaks running from each eye; the upper streak stretches towards a black patch on the neck. The belly is yellowish to pale brown, and each ventral scale is spotted with brown. The scales along the middle of the back, called the vertebral scales, are slightly enlarged and keeled. The Keeled Slug Snake inhabits damp, well-watered places where its prey abounds. It seizes a snail in its soft body, and forcibly draws it out of its shell by alternate movements of its jaws. It is nocturnal, and reproduces by laying eggs. The young are said to mature in less than a year. Adults are about 60 cm long.

Sub-family Colubrinae
Genera Elaphe and Gonyosoma (Racers)

Five species under the genus Elaphe and one under the genus Gonyosoma are distributed in this region. They occur in varying habitats, and being diurnal, are hence, commonly encountered in the field.

Genus Elaphe

Common Racer
Elaphe flavolineata

Non-venomous

Young Common Racer in striking attitude

The Common Racer is a fairly large snake. It is equally at home on the ground as well as in the trees. It feeds on a wide variety of prey, for example, rodents, birds and amphibians. The snake subdues the prey by seizing it in its mouth, and holding it down with the constricting coils of its body. The Common Racer is usually encountered in open country, and plays a valuable role in the control of the population of harmful rodents. When cornered, it rears up its coiled forebody in anticipation of a strike. The young sometimes enter gardens in search of lizards and other small prey. When fully grown, the Common Racer reaches a length of about 2 m.

Copperhead Racer
Elaphe radiata

Non-venomous

This is a strikingly beautiful snake of about 2 m in length that commonly occurs in open country and grasslands. It is a courageous snake and will stand its ground even against a larger opponent. When molested, it coils up its laterally flattened neck and gets ready to strike with a gaping mouth. Birds and rats are its usual prey and being widely distributed, its occurrence in Singapore and the northern states of Peninsular Malaysia has been recorded. Copperhead Racers reproduce by laying eggs which are deposited in holes in the ground.

Copperhead Racer in defensive posture

Striped Racer
Elaphe taeniura

Non-venomous

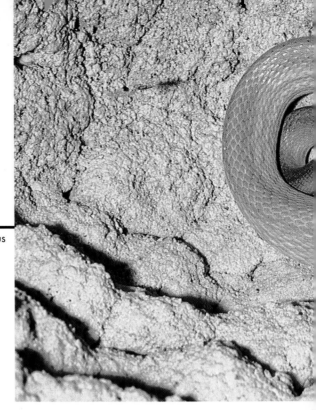

This is a fairly common snake of up to 2 m in length. It is easily recognisable by the distinct longitudinal white and black stripes on the posterior part of its body. There seems to be some colour variation that co-relates to habitat preferences and range: Striped Racers occurring in the open and woodlands tend to be darker while those found in limestone caves tend to be of a lighter hue.

This snake has a wide geographical distribution, ranging from the eastern Himalayas to Burma, China, Thailand, Sumatra and Taiwan. In parts of its range, it is hunted as a delicacy and its skin is extensively used in the leather trade. The Striped Racer is also distributed in the northern half of Peninsular Malaysia, particularly in limestone hills. It moves swiftly, climbs well and hunts for small mammals, which it kills by constriction. Striped Racers that inhabit dark caves feed mainly on bats.

Striped Racers reproduce by laying eggs, which are said to number from 11 to 13 per clutch. The eggs are usually deposited in late June and early July (*Fitch, 1970*).

Striped Racer

Red-tailed Racer

Genus Gonyosoma

Red-tailed Racer
Non-venomous
Gonyosoma oxycephalum

This largely arboreal and diurnal snake gets its name from its reddish or rusty brown tail. Its body is a beautiful green, and the snake is quite hard to spot among the foliage of its jungle habitat. It feeds on small mammals and birds, and rests on branches with its head in the centre of its coils. The Red-tailed Racer reproduces by laying eggs; the eggs are said to take about $3\frac{1}{2}$ to over 4 months to hatch. One one-metre-long Red-tailed Racer was recorded to lay 7 infertile eggs over a few days in late September. The eggs averaged about 65 mm long and are very elongated. The young Red-tailed Racer is olive brown in colour with narrow, oblique white bars on the posterior part of its body. When fully grown, it can attain a length of about 2 m.

41

Genera Zaocys and Ptyas (Rat Snakes)

These are diurnal snakes that feed mainly on rodents, and are therefore called rat snakes. They are fast-moving, and one species, the Keeled Rat Snake, has the distinction of being the largest of the land Colubrine snakes, attaining a length of about 4 m.

Genus Zaocys

Keeled Rat Snake
Zaocys carinatus   Non-venomous

The Keeled Rat Snake, sometimes known as the Keel-back Rat Snake, somewhat resembles the deadly King Cobra in appearance. When disturbed, the Keeled Rat Snake often raises its forebody vertically in a striking posture that is similar to that of a disturbed King Cobra except that the Keeled Rat Snake has no hood. These rat snakes inhabit lowland jungles and open country as well as close to human settlements where amphibians and rodents abound. Young Keeled Rat Snakes are often found with amphibians in their stomachs. Each clutch comprises about 10 eggs which take about 2 months to hatch.

In spite of its name, the Indo-Chinese Rat Snake relishes frogs as well.

Genus Ptyas

Indo-Chinese Rat Snake
Ptyas korros

Non-venomous

Like all rat snakes, this snake does man a good service by feeding on rodent pests, which it seizes and holds down with its body coils till they are subdued. The name "Indo-Chinese Rat Snake" is a misnomer as it is fairly common and distributed widely throughout Southeast Asia. It was observed that the snake has arboreal tendencies, and will climb trees where it often rests. Mating is also said to take place in the trees. About 4 to 9 eggs are laid; one snake laid 5 elongated eggs in early June, and the young emerged after an incubation period of 61 days. Newly hatched Indo-Chinese Rat Snakes measure about 290 mm long. It is believed that the Indo-Chinese Rat Snake can breed more than once a year. Adult Indo-Chinese Rat Snakes are about 2 m long.

The newly hatched Indo-Chinese Rat Snake looks like its parents.

Banded Rat Snake
Ptyas mucosus

Non-venomous

This large-eyed rat snake grows to a length of 2.3 m, but is said to attain a record length of about 4 m! It is mainly terrestrial and hunts for small mammals and birds, as well as amphibians and other snakes, in wooded areas and plantations. The snake subdues the prey by pressing it against the ground with its stout body. Being large, it possesses a fierce temper when cornered, and retaliates by inflating itself with air, which is then forced out, thus creating a growling sound which can be heard some distance away. About 9 to18 eggs are laid, each measuring about 50 mm long. The female coils around the eggs and guards them. The eggs hatch in about 60 days. Young Banded Rat Snakes feed mainly on small lizards and amphibians till they are old enough to tackle rodents. These young rat snakes have light-coloured crossbands on the forepart of their bodies. Tweedie (1983) did not include this species in his list of Malayan snakes. In recent years, two specimens of rat snakes that looked and behaved like *P. mucosus* had been collected in Singapore. Further field collections are needed to confirm its occurrence there.

Genus Xenelaphis (Brown Snakes)

There are two species of snakes under this genus, which occur in the Malaysian region. The Ocellated Brown Snake (*X. ellipsifer*) is the rarer of the two.

Malayan Brown Snake
Xenelaphis hexagonotus

Non-venomous

This is a terrestrial snake found in cultivated areas and plantations where it is considered a valuable predator of rodent pests. It also takes fish and amphibians. The young Malayan Brown Snake is of a light brown, ground colour with dark crossbars on the forepart of its body which is remarkably cylindrical. The colour becomes darker in the adult snake. The scales on its tail are edged with black, and its underside is yellow.

It is said to be common and grows to a length of between 1.6 and 2 m. One captive Malayan Brown Snake laid 7 eggs in a rock hollow in early October. The eggs averaged about 60 mm in length and 23 mm in diameter.

The Malayan Brown Snake is a valuable predator of rodent pests.

Striped Kukri Snake

Brown Kukri Snake

Genus Oligodon (Kukris)

These are relatively small terrestrial snakes with secretive habits. Kukri snakes are so called because the rear teeth of their upper jaw resemble the blade of the Gurkha's kukri. They are strikingly coloured and patterned, and of the 3 species occurring in this region, 2 are described here.

Striped Kukri Snake
Oligodon octolineatus

Non-venomous

This is an extremely beautiful snake of about 60 cm in length. It is commonly found in gardens and cultivated areas. Being generally inoffensive, it prefers to mind its own business. However, if it is provoked, it has the curious habit of hiding its head under its coils and raising and waving its tail to reveal the coral pink undersides. It also discharges an objectionable odour. Breeding seems to occur all year round. One 7-cm-long snake laid 5 eggs in early May — the eggs measured about 30 mm in length and 16 mm in diameter. Another Striped Kukri Snake was recorded to lay 4 eggs in early October. In the wild, eggs are often deposited in soil, and in piles of vegetable debris and sawdust. Adult Striped Kukri Snakes feed on small animals, like lizards and frogs, as well as other snakes, and are also known to relish frog spawn and bird eggs.

Brown Kukri Snake
Oligodon purpurascens

Non-venomous

The Brown Kukri Snake is common in wooded country. It seems to possess a gentle disposition and seldom attempts to bite. In captivity, it relishes raw eggs beaten and served in a shallow dish. The snake readily drinks up the liquid until none is left. Young Brown Kukri Snakes are brightly coloured and, when fully grown, can attain a length of about 90 cm. Nothing much is known about its reproductive habits.

Brightly-coloured juvenile Brown Kukri Snake

Genus Calamaria
(Reed Snakes)

In this region, there are 5 genera of rather obscure, small, burrowing reed snakes so called because of their cylindrical bodies and short tails. Owing to their size and secretive habits, reed snakes are rarely seen. The snakes get their name from "calamus" which means "reed", an apt reference to their appearance.

Variable Reed Snake
Calamaria lumbricoidea

Non-venomous

Variable Reed Snakes are said to be of two distinct colour variations, which may be associated with altitudes. The mountain variety, which occurs from 1 000 m above sea level, is dark brown above with a belly distinctly marked or barred with yellow and black. Each of the body scales is edged with white above and below. The lowland variety is pictured here.

The tail ends in a sharp point for both varieties. Variable Reed Snakes feed on small prev, like insects and skinks. When fully gro Variable Reed Snake is about 40 cm long the largest of the reed snakes found in region. The highland variety is widely distributed, whereas the lowland variety seems to be uncommon.

Pink-headed Reed Snake
Calamaria schlegeli schlegeli

Non-venomous

This fascinating snake is immediately recognisable by its bright pink head and small, black, beady eyes. It is found in lowland forests, where it hides under stones, logs or clumps of vegetation. Small animals, like slugs and frogs, form its usual diet. An adult Pink-headed Reed Snake is about 38 cm long. Nothing much is known about its breeding habits other than it lays eggs. One 13-cm-long young Pink-headed Reed Snake was collected from under a leaf in mid-December. It looked similar to the adult except that it had black bands over the posterior half of its light-coloured belly. Peninsular Malaysian specimens may have the head partly or wholly black instead of pink (*Tweedie, 1983*). A distinct sub-species of the Pink-headed Reed Snake is said to be found in Java.

Found in lowland forests, the Pink-headed Reed Snake often hides under stones, logs or leaf litter.

49

Genus Pseudorhabdion

Dwarf Reed Snake
Pseudorhabdion longiceps

Non-venomous

This is a small, burrowing snake that lives under stones, fallen logs and damp piles of decaying vegetation. It feeds mainly on small insects and their larvae, and can grow up to 23 cm long although the usual length is about 10 to 17 cm. The snake's tail is short and pointed; the male has a longer tail than the female. The Dwarf Reed Snake is sometimes mistaken for the Common Blind Snake, but a closer look at the former will reveal the presence of eyes and belly scales. The Dwarf Reed Snake may or may not possess a yellow ring and a pair of light spots on the head. Dwarf Reed Snakes are commonly encountered on the forest floor. They are completely harmless.

The Dwarf Reed Snake is sometimes mistaken for the Common Blind Snake.

Orange-bellied Snake — variable form

Genus Liopeltis

Orange-bellied Snake
Liopeltis baliodeira

Non-venomous

Like other species under the genus, the habits and biology of this snake are little known. The coloration and markings on its body are said to be variable, and may range from reddish to dark brown, with dark-edged yellow or light-coloured spots on its neck and the anterior part of its body. Its belly is light orange in colour. It grows to about 30 to 45 cm long and is found in lowland forests.

Two specimens of what appeared to be the variable form of *L. baliodeira* have been collected in Singapore in recent years. Though their scale counts are consistent with the normal form, further studies are needed to confirm their true identity.

Orange-bellied Snake — normal form

Genus Dendrelaphis (Bronzebacks)

This genus comprises slender, distinctly coloured snakes which are diurnal as well as arboreal. They are very active among the branches, being able to climb vertically with speed and ease: they have keeled ventral scales to help them in climbing. Their eyes are rather large. The bronzeback is so called because of the bronze colour on its back. Of the 4 species found in this region, 3 are described here.

Painted Bronzeback
Dendrelaphis pictus

Non-venomous

This is a very common snake of lowland jungles. It is also usually encountered in open country and gardens, where it hunts for small prey, like frogs and lizards. It is usually mild-mannered, but when provoked, it will inflate its forebody to reveal the bright green or bluish spots on the skin in between the scales. When roughly handled, it may omit a foul-smelling odour from its glands. Painted Bronzebacks breed all the year round, laying between 4 and 6 eggs in a clutch. One 84-cm-long snake laid 4 eggs in late September and another 85-cm-long specimen was recorded to lay 5 eggs in late February. The eggs averaged 33 mm in length and 10 mm in diameter. The incubation period is about 75 to 76 days, and the newly hatched snakes are about 280 mm long and appear similar to the adults in coloration.

The Painted Bronzeback employs its speed and keen eyesight to hunt its prey.

Elegant Bronzeback
Dendrelaphis formosus

Non-venomous

This is an elegantly coloured snake which occurs mainly in lowland jungles, and appears to be less common than the Painted Bronzeback. The reddish patch on its neck becomes very distinct when it puffs up in a defensive posture. Its eyes are large, and a broad, black streak runs from the snout through the eyes and onto the neck. This courageous snake has been observed to tackle and eventually subdue tough and difficult prey, like the Green Tree Lizard. It lays up to 8 eggs in a clutch, and the young emerge in about 92 days. The newly hatched snakes are between 270 and 300 mm long. When mature, the Elegant Bronzeback reaches a length of about 1.2 m.

The Elegant Bronzeback hunts in the day for lizards and birds.

The Striped Bronzeback is among the largest of its genus found in this region.

Striped Bronzeback
Dendrelaphis caudolineatus

Non-venomous

This pretty, tree-dwelling snake grows up to 2 m, and feeds mainly on tree-lizards, frogs and small birds. It is fairly common in forests, wooded areas and near human settlements. In captivity, the Striped Bronzeback can be coaxed to feed on house lizards and fish. The prey is seized immediately and swallowed quickly. One wild Striped Bronzeback which was captured, laid 5 eggs in mid-July. The eggs were very elongated and measured 48 mm in length and 12 mm in diameter. Another wild 1.2-m-long specimen laid 8 eggs in early November. The eggs hatched in 54 days, and the newly hatched snakes measured about 340 mm long.

The Common House Snake often enters houses to hunt for its favourite prey — the house lizards.

Genus Lycodon (Wolf Snakes)

This group of snakes are nocturnal and possess enlarged front teeth in the upper jaw, but these are not venom fangs. The name "Wolf Snake" is rather a misnomer since these snakes are not at all fierce as their name suggests. There are 5 species of wolf snakes occurring in this region, 3 of which are described here.

Common House Snake or Wolf Snake
Lycodon aulicus

Non-venomous

Several sub-species of this snake have been recorded, largely owing to its wide geographical distribution. It possesses remarkable climbing abilities, and often lives in cracks and crevices of walls or timber in buildings, where its favourite prey, the house lizard, abounds. The prey is seized by the head and held in the snake's coils till it is finally subdued. About 3 – 11 eggs are laid, and the young hatch from the eggs after an incubation period of $1\frac{1}{2}$ months. Baby House Snakes look similar to the adult snakes and they feed on tiny lizards. The House Snake can reach a length of about 50 cm.

54

Scarce Wolf Snake
Lycodon effraenis

Non-venomous

This uncommon snake is found distributed throughout Peninsular Malaysia. It seems to frequent human settlements, and the specimen pictured here was discovered in a pile of fire-wood in Kuala Tahan, Pahang Darul Makmur, Malaysia. Small lizards and other snakes probably form its usual prey, and the adult Scarce Wolf Snake reaches a length of about 60 to 90 cm. Nothing much is known about its breeding habits.

The rare Scarce Wolf Snake occurs in lowland forests, and can climb well.

Indo-Chinese Wolf Snake
Lycodon laoensis

Non-venomous

The Indo-Chinese Wolf Snake, as the name implies, is found mainly in Thailand and Indo-China. However, it has been recorded in the Malaysian state of Kelantan Darul Naim. It grows to a length of about 45 cm, and feeds on lizards and skinks, as well as other snakes. About 5 eggs are laid in a clutch.

The Indo-Chinese Wolf Snake is probably the most beautiful of its genus.

Genus Sibynophis (Collared Snakes)

A genus represented by two species that possess scale characteristics similar to those of the Wolf Snakes, but are immediately distinguished by their tiny and numerous closely-set teeth. Only 1 species is described here and the Black-headed Collared Snake is a name suggested by Francis L.K. Lim.

Black-headed Collared Snake
Sibynophis melanocephalus

Non-venomous

This relatively obscure ground snake inhabits lowland areas, where it hunts for skinks among the grass and bushes. It is fairly common and widely distributed, and grows to a length of about 60 cm. Nothing much is known except that it is diurnal, and reproduces by laying eggs.

Sub-family Natricinae (Keelbacks)

This sub-family is one of the largest and most widely-distributed groups of Colubrine snakes, being found in Southeast Asia, North and Central America, most of Europe, and northern and western Africa. In Europe, they are commonly referred to as Grass Snakes. The markedly keeled body scales are normally characteristic of this group of snakes, hence the name, keelbacks. In this region, a dozen or so species occur which are represented by 7 genera, of which 4 species represented by 3 genera are described here.

Genus Xenochrophis

Chequered Keelback
Xenochrophis piscator

Non-venomous

The Chequered Keelback is a water-loving snake commonly found near ponds, streams and in paddy fields throughout Peninsular Malaysia. It is adapted to an aquatic way of life: it has upturned nostrils, and is able to swim well. It is also equally at home on land. Frogs and fish form its normal diet. Though the Chequered Keelback is non-venomous, it is capable of giving a nasty bite if roughly handled. It seems to breed throughout the year, and being a prolific breeder, lays from 20 to over 80 eggs in a clutch! However, the average number in a clutch is about 40. The eggs hatch in about 2 to $2\frac{1}{2}$ months and the hatchlings are about 110 mm long. The adult snake is about 1.2 m long. In Singapore, the Chequered Keelback is, in all probability, an introduced species.

The Chequered Keelback feeds on fish, and is a prolific breeder, laying up to 80 eggs in a clutch.

Four specimens of this Striped Keelback have been collected in Singapore in recent years.

Striped Keelback
Xenochrophis vittatus

Non-venomous

Head of Striped Keelback

This Striped Keelback is an inhabitant of grassy and wet areas, where it hunts for fish and amphibians. It possesses enlarged rear teeth in the upper jaw, but they are not venom fangs. The enlarged teeth probably aid the snake when it seizes slippery and struggling prey. It is also a remarkable breeder, having been recorded to lay up to 2 clutches of between 5 and 8 eggs annually. The hatchlings are said to mature in about 11 months! (Most snakes mature in 2 to 3 years.) Adults are about 70 cm long.

The Striped Keelback occurs in Sumatra and Java, and 4 specimens have been collected in Singapore so far. The British Museum (*1982*) in commenting that these could be the first records of the Striped Keelback occurring in Singapore, propounded that the snakes could have been imported or escaped pets. Hence, further field studies are needed to ascertain the species status in Singapore.

Genus Rhabdophis

Red-necked Keelback
Rhabdophis subminiatus

Non-venomous

This Red-necked Keelback is easily recognised by the reddish patch on its neck. Its body is uniformly olive or brown, with dark spots or reticulations. There is a black streak running from the eye to the upper lips. The scales on its body are all moderately keeled.

The Red-necked Keelback is recorded mainly in the northern parts of Peninsular Malaysia, Thailand and south China. It inhabits montane forests, hills and lowland areas, particularly near streams or rivers, where it preys on amphibians and fish. It does not appear to be as aggressive as the Chequered Keelback (X. piscator), but care should be taken when handling the Red-necked Keelback as it has been known to seriously injure its handler with its bite. The last pair of teeth in the upper jaw are greatly enlarged but not grooved, and the saliva may be potent in some specimens. When molested, the Red-necked Keelback sometimes flattens its body and jerks about.

The little that is known about the Red-necked Keelback's reproduction showed that it is not as prolific as the Chequered Keelback. Two clutches of 8 eggs were laid in mid-January, and one 78-cm-long snake had 14 eggs in her oviducts. The eggs averaged 25 mm in length and 12 mm in diameter. Newly hatched snakes have large heads and eyes, as well as a conspicuous black and yellowish orange crossbar on the neck, and they emerge after an incubation period of 50 days. Fully-grown Red-necked Keelbacks are about 80 cm in length.

The Red-necked Keelback has been known to seriously injure its handler with its bite.

Genus Macropisthodon

Snakes of this genus are distinguished from the other Natricine snakes by their greatly enlarged last two maxillary teeth.

Blue-necked Keelback
Macropisthodon rhodomelas

Non-venomous

Juvenile Red-necked Keelback

This is a small, common snake of the lowlands, and is frequently found close to the water's edge. When disturbed, the Blue-necked Keelback will rear up and flatten its neck like the cobra. A whitish discharge, secreted by glands under the skin, oozes onto the blue patch of the neck — the purpose of this phenomenon is still a mystery. The adult Blue-necked Keelbacks feed on frogs, and young snakes are said to eat tadpoles. They grow to a length of between 30 and 60 cm.

Back-fanged Mildly Venomous Snakes

Genus Chrysopelea (Tree Snakes)

These diurnal, active tree-living snakes differ from the bronzebacks in having back fangs, that is, grooved poison fangs at the rear of the upper jaw. Their venom, however, is weak and not dangerous to man. Their belly scales are keeled and notched as in the bronzebacks. Snakes of this genus also possess the unique ability to glide from tree to tree: they launch themselves from a high branch, and then flatten and hollow their ventral scales so as to trap a cushion of air underneath in the same manner as a parachute would. Of the 5 species belonging to this genus, 3 occur in this region.

Paradise Tree Snake
Chrysopelea paradisi

Mildly venomous

This snake is commonly found in the forests as well as in gardens, where it may occasionally enter houses to feed on house lizards. Its diet also includes small birds and mice, as well as tree-living lizards, like flying dragons. The snake seizes and holds down the prey with its coils till its weak venom takes effect. One specimen caught in the wild had the remains of a finch-like bird in its stomach. About 5 to 8 eggs are laid in a clutch; the eggs are white, elongated and cylindrical, and average about 35 to 40 mm in length and 10 mm in diameter. The Paradise Tree Snake may or may not possess a row of four-petalled bright red spots along the middle of the back. It grows to a length of 1.2 m.

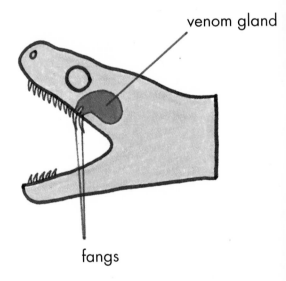

venom gland

fangs

Position of fangs and venom gland
in back-fanged snakes

Paradise Tree Snakes may or may not possess a row of four-petalled bright red spots along the middle of the back.

Golden Tree Snake
Chrysopelea ornata

Mildly venomous

The eggs hatch in
about 65 days

The Golden Tree Snake normally occurs in the northern states of Peninsular Malaysia where it inhabits forested hills. It is slightly longer than the Paradise Tree Snake, growing up to 1.5 m. Its feeding habits are similar to those of other tree snakes: lizards and small birds are said to be eaten alive. Up to 10 eggs are laid, and these hatch in about 65 days. The newly hatched snakes look similar to the adults, and average 260 mm in length.

Being an excellent climber, the Golden Tree Snake
hunts for prey in its arboreal habitat.

Twin-barred Tree Snake
Chrysopelea pelias

Mildly venomous

This is a very colourful, but rare tree snake with habits similar to those of the Paradise Tree Snake and the Golden Tree Snake. It grows to a length of 60 to 70 cm, and occurs in forests. Distributed widely in this region, it is also found in Singapore. Nothing much is known about this beautiful snake and its reproduction.

The Oriental Whip Snake in a life-and-death struggle with an agamid (lizard).

Genus Ahaetulla; Dryophiops (Whip Snakes)

These are generally called whip snakes as they have exceedingly slender bodies, spear-shaped heads with pointed snouts and horizontally elongated pupils. These snakes are back-fanged, and produce live young.

The Oriental Whip Snake is mainly tree-bound.

Oriental Whip Snake
Ahaetulla prasina

Mildly venomous

The long, thin body of this snake is usually deep green, but light-coloured forms also occur. The belly is pale green and marked by a yellow stripe along each side. Found in wooded areas and being mainly tree-bound, the Oriental Whip Snake sometimes travels short distances over the ground. It is also found in gardens, and sometimes enters houses through open windows. One should not panic if one encounters an Oriental Whip Snake as it is normally gentle, and can be picked up with little risk of being bitten. It feeds on small birds and lizards, and has the curious habit of sticking out its tongue for a long time. About 4 to 6 young are born in a litter, and they are light brown in colour. The young feed on flies and small lizards, and attain a length of about 2 m when fully grown. Oriental Whip Snakes are commonly distributed in Singapore and Peninsular Malaysia.

Long-nosed Whip Snake
Ahaetulla nasuta

Mildly venomous

It is so called because of the extended piece of skin on its snout. Found mainly in trees and bushes, it feeds on lizards and amphibians. In captivity, the Long-nosed Whip Snake feeds readily on house geckos, and is quite popular as a pet. The adult snake is about 90 cm to 1 m long. It is usually green, but other colour forms can also be found. These colour forms range from tan to brownish grey and golden. The size of each litter ranges from 3 to as many as 22 young. One Long-nosed Whip Snake was recorded to give birth to 6 babies in late September. The newborn snakes are green in colour and average 39 cm long. The Long-nosed Whip Snake occurs mainly in the northern part of Southeast Asia.

Keel-bellied Whip Snake

Keel-bellied Whip Snake
Dryophiops rubescens

Mildly venomous

This is an uncommon snake of between 1 and 1.2 m long. It has acute eyesight that enables it to seek out elusive prey among its leafy habitat. Its habits and reproduction are probably similar to those of other whip snakes found in this region. The Keel-bellied Whip Snake occurs in the southern half of Peninsular Malaysia and has been found in Singapore.

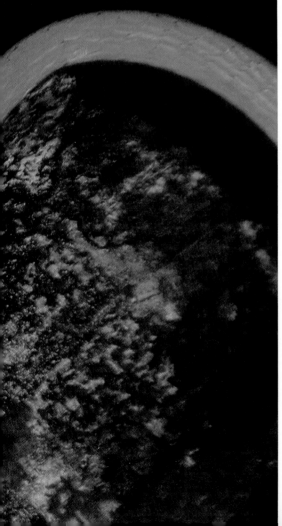

Long-nosed Whip Snake

Sub-family Homalopsinae (Water Snakes)

Snakes belonging to this sub-family are represented by 7 genera with about a dozen species distributed throughout the Singapore and Peninsular Malaysia region. They are all fresh or tidal water snakes, and the commonest of these are the Puff-faced Water Snake and the Dog-faced Water Snake. These snakes produce live young. They are all back-fanged and hence, mildly-venomous. Four genera and 6 species are described here.

The baby Puff-faced Water Snake is vividly coloured.

Genus Homalopsis

Puff-faced Water Snake
Homalopsis buccata

Mildly venomous

This water snake has markedly keeled scales on its body. It inhabits both fresh and slightly brackish water in coastal areas. It is specially adapted for an aquatic way of life: its nostrils are situated on top of the snout, and its eyes lie near the top of the head. Though its venom is considered weak and insignificant, it has a vicious temper, and will bite severely if roughly handled or accidentally trodden upon. It is considered a pest on fish farms due to its predilection for fish. This snake grows to a little over 1 m in length. One Puff-faced Water Snake had 7 fully developed embryos in late April. The embryos averaged 230 mm long.

The Dog-faced Water Snake hides in holes during the day, and comes out to hunt at night.

Genus Cerberus

Dog-faced Water Snake
Cerberus rhynchops

Mildly venomous

This is a one-metre-long snake occurring in brackish ponds, mangrove swamps as well as in muddy coastal creeks. It feeds mainly on fish, which it seizes in its mouth and quickly swallows. The snake's skin is said to be used for making ornamental leather goods. It is nocturnal and possesses a remarkable side-winding capability that enables it to move across mud flats with relative ease. About 6 to 30 young are born in a litter and are said to remain together for a while before dispersing.

Genus Enhydris

There are 6 species of these water snakes in Peninsular Malaysia, 3 of which are described here. They differ from the other groups of water snakes in that they have smooth scales on their bodies.

Bocourt's Water Snake
Enhydris bocourti

Mildly venomous

This snake is found commonly in freshwater streams in hilly habitats of the northern states of Peninsular Malaysia. It is the largest of all the water snakes belonging to the genus *Enhydris*, with full-grown specimens reaching up to 1 m in length. Its body is stout, and the colour and patterns are not as bright and vivid as those of a young snake of the same species. Fish and frogs form its diet, the prey being seized in the mouth and immobilised by the venom from its back fangs. The snake produces live young, and a litter may number up to 17. The newborn snakes are about 220 mm in length.

The stout-bodied Bocourt's Water Snake grows to about 1 m long.

A Plumbeous Water Snake feeding on a small tilapia (fish).

Plumbeous Water Snake
Enhydris plumbea

Mildly venomous

This stout-bodied snake grows to a length of 35 – 48 cm. Its body is of a drab olive colour, which contrasts with its yellowish undersides. Largely aquatic by nature, it is found in ditches, ponds, streams and even in estuaries, where it preys on fish and amphibians. The reproductive season is said to be from June to November, and the number of young in each litter ranges from 6 to 30. Baby Plumbeous Water Snakes measure 75 to 115 mm long, and are greenish in colour. This snake is commonly distributed in the northern states of Peninsular Malaysia and has been recorded as far south as Malacca.

Rainbow Water Snake
Enhydris enhydris

Mildly venomous

This is a beautiful freshwater snake found in coastal rivers, where it feeds on fish and frogs. Though its head seems small, it is capable of swallowing large, slippery prey. Its breeding season is reportedly long, and the size of each litter ranges from 10 to 18 young. It grows to about 60 cm long, but the usual length is less than this. The Rainbow Water Snake is commonly distributed in the northern states of Peninsular Malaysia, but it has been recorded in Singapore as well.

73

Genus Herpeton

Tentacled Snake
Herpeton tentaculatum

Mildly venomous

This snake is easily identifiable by its moderately thick body, markedly keeled scales, and a pair of tentacles or scaly appendages on its snout. It is believed that the snake uses its tentacles as decoys or lures to attract unsuspecting fish to swim within striking range. It inhabits slow-moving streams, where it usually remains still with its tail coiled around a submerged object, like a plant or a tree root. It assumes a rigid posture when molested. Up to 10 young are born in a litter. The Tentacled Snake grows up to a length of 75 cm. It is distributed in Thailand and Indo-China.

The pair of scaly tentacles on the snout may be a lure to attract fish.

Mock Viper

Genus Psammodynastes (Mock Vipers)

This genus has only 2 known species occurring in Malaysia. They are back-fanged, and possess an irritable disposition. One species is described here.

Mock Viper
Psammodynastes pulverulentus

Mildly venomous

This active little snake is pugnacious and will bite readily if disturbed. It occurs in wooded areas in the lowlands and montane country of up to 1 000 m above sea level. Equally at home on the ground as well as in the trees, it preys on amphibians and lizards. Being widely distributed, several colour forms are known, ranging from dark brown to reddish brown and grey, with dark spots or obscure markings. The Mock Viper is said to breed throughout the year, and it bears live young in a litter numbering from 3 to 10 young. When fully grown, the Mock Viper is about 60 cm long.

75

Mangrove Snake in a dramatic striking posture.

Genus Boiga
(Cat Snakes)

Snakes belonging to this group are generally known as cat snakes because of their vertical slit-like pupils which resemble those of a cat's eyes. These snakes are fairly large, arboreal and nocturnal. The head is broader than the neck, and the body is long and usually laterally flattened. The poste- rior teeth of the upper jaws are enlarged and grooved to act as poison fangs. Of the 5 species of cat snakes known to occur in Singapore and Peninsular Malaysia, 4 species are described here.

Mangrove Snake
Boiga dendrophila melanota

Mildly venomous

This handsome snake occurs mainly in lowland jungles and mangrove swamps. Its bluish-black body is marked by 40 to 50 narrow, yellow crossbars. Various sub-species have been recorded and the one described here is found in Malaysia and east Sumatra. Its colour pattern is reminiscent of that of the deadly venomous Banded Krait (*Bungarus fasciatus*), though in the latter, the black and yellow bands are of more or less equal width. The Mangrove Snake rests coiled up among the branches which span over streams or rivers, and becomes active at dusk when it hunts for birds and eggs as well as rodents. Its usually docile nature makes it a favourite among snake charmers. However, when provoked, it will bite with little warning. About 4 to 15 eggs are laid per clutch, and the incubation period is about 3 months. One captive Mangrove Snake was recorded to deposit 3 clutches totalling 25 eggs over a 12-month period. Newly hatched Mangrove Snakes are about 340 mm long and resemble the adult in coloration, except for the pinkish or orange rings on the hatchlings' tails. When mature, the Mangrove Snake reaches a length of about 2.5 m.

White-spotted Cat Snake
Boiga drapiezii

Mildly venomous

This is a relatively long cat snake, reaching a length of 2.1 m. There are sometimes variations in body coloration and this may be associated with age. It is generally mild-mannered, and rarely attempts to bite when handled. Birds, eggs and other small prey form its usual diet. Nothing much is known about this rare cat snake except that it occurs mainly in the southern portion of Peninsular Malaysia, and that it has the habit of depositing its eggs in the nest of tree-dwelling termites, where the consistently warm temperature helps incubate its eggs.

The rare White-spotted Cat Snake deposits its eggs in the nests of tree-dwelling termites.

Dog-toothed Cat Snake
Boiga cynodon

Mildly venomous

The Dog-toothed Cat Snake exists in two colour forms of which the melanistic variety is uncommon. It is an exceedingly good climber. It is capable of stretching its slender and laterally flattened body into space to reach a distant branch. Its tail is strong and prehensile. Being nocturnal, it hunts for birds and their eggs at dusk. Observations on the reproduction of captive Dog-toothed Cat Snakes indicated that breeding occurs throughout the year. The eggs are white and elongated, and are deposited in the months of early February and May, June, mid-July, September, late October and mid-November. Preliminary studies of the frequency of laying showed that the Dog-toothed Cat Snake lays more than one clutch, and possibly up to three clutches of eggs annually. A clutch may number from 6 to 12 eggs, and the incubation period is $2\frac{1}{2}$ months or longer. The adult Dog-toothed Cat Snake reaches a length of about 3 m, and is widely found in forests.

The Dog-toothed Cat Snake prefers dry wooded forests, and is a good climber.

The Jasper Cat Snake puffs its neck up in defensive display.

Jasper Cat Snake
Boiga jaspidea

Mildly venomous

This is a rather rare cat snake growing to a maximum length of about 1.4 m. The intricate pattern of spots and bars on its body, as well as the symmetrical arrangement of black, light-bordered spots on the head, makes this snake easily recognisable from the other cat snakes of the same genus. Largely arboreal, the Jasper Cat Snake occurs in lowland jungles as well as in higher altitudes. It feeds on small animals, like birds and mice, and on one occasion, a 1.2- m-long Jasper Cat Snake which was caught in the Singapore Zoo had 3 bird eggshells in its stomach. Nothing much is known about its reproduction though it is said to deposit its eggs in the nest of tree termites. In early December, a 51-cm-long Jasper Cat Snake was collected in the zoo's grounds. The young specimen looked similar to the adult. When at rest, the young Jasper Cat Snake coiled itself up in a tight circle, with its head in the centre.

The Green Cat-eyed Snake in a striking attitude.

The Green Cat-eyed Snake has a long and slender, green body.

Green Cat-eyed Snake
Boiga cyanea

Mildly venomous

The adult Green Cat-eyed Snake is about 1.65 m long and is found in Burma and Indo-China. At first glance, this snake looks similar to the Oriental Whip Snake because of its green and long body. However, the belly of a Green Cat-eyed Snake is of a lighter green; it could also be greenish white or yellow. Its throat is bluish white and the inside of its mouth is blue-black. This snake is commonly found in trees with branches spanning the water, and it preys on mice, birds, lizards and other snakes. The prey is killed by a combination of constriction and venomous bite.

Front-fanged Venomous Snakes

Family Elapidae

Snakes belonging to this family have rigid fangs in the anterior part of the upper jaw. The hollow fangs are used to inject venom in a manner like that of a hypodermic syringe. Most species in this family are highly venomous and are thus considered dangerous to man.

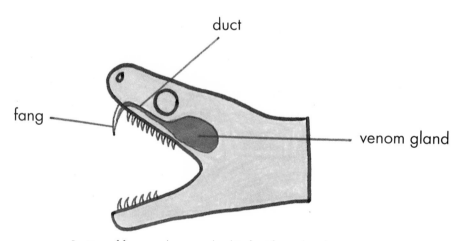

Position of fangs and venom gland in front-fanged snakes

Genus Maticora (Coral Snakes)

These are relatively small but brightly-coloured, burrowing elapids. They are mainly nocturnal and are generally considered non-aggressive unless roughly handled. Their mouths are small and generally believed to be incapable of inflicting an effective bite on an adult human. Little is known of the venom and hence, these snakes should be treated with caution. The venom glands are extraordinary in that they extend way back to about one third or more of the snake's body length.

Blue Coral Snake
Maticora bivirgata

Venomous

This is a relatively long and slender-bodied snake. It inhabits the lowland forests of Singapore and Peninsular Malaysia, where it is said to be quite common. The Blue Coral Snake feeds almost exclusively on other snakes, including smaller members of its kind. It reacts in a way similar to the kukri snakes when disturbed: it tucks its head under its coils and raises its tail to reveal its startling coral red belly. It will bite if handled, and the consequences can be rapidly fatal. There are 2 known fatalities highly suspected to have been caused by the Blue Coral Snake: one in which a young child died 2 hours after being bitten in the web of the skin at the base of the thumb in 1956; the other in which a man died within 5 minutes after being bitten twice on his left toes in 1985. This beautiful snake does not seem to thrive well in captivity. Not much is known about its breeding habits. A full-grown Blue Coral Snake can reach a length of about 1.5 m.

Banded Coral Snake
Maticora intestinalis

Venomous

This is a small, secretive, burrowing snake. It is usually found living in piles of decaying leaf litter on the forest floor, as well as in loose soil, where it is sometimes accidentally unearthed during gardening work. The underside of this snake is pale-coloured and marked with numerous black crossbands. The adult Banded Coral Snake is about 60 cm long. One specimen caught in the wild was observed to writhe about, raising its tail end when disturbed. It later regurgitated a dead Common Blind Snake. When encountered in the field, the snake should never be handled with bare hands as a severe, but fortunately, non-fatal case of a Banded Coral Snake bite had been recorded. It is widely distributed in Singapore as well as in Malaysia, where a dark-coloured mountain form has been found besides the normal form.

Genus Bungarus (Kraits)

These are generally large elapine snakes of mild and sluggish temperament. All the snakes belonging to this group are called kraits. They are nocturnal and venomous. Cases of fatal bites by some species of this group have been recorded. The venom acts chiefly as a neurotoxin. All the 3 species found in this region are described here.

Banded Krait
Bungarus fasciatus

Venomous

The body of this krait is somewhat ridged and triangular in cross-section. Its stumpy tail is banded black and yellow like its body. It seems to be quite docile in the daytime, and may even be handled with little risk of the handler being bitten. However, at night, it becomes bold and unpredictable. It feeds almost exclusively on other snakes, namely baby pythons, whip snakes, rat snakes and bronzebacks. One Banded Krait in the Madras Snake Farm, India, was reported to have laid 12 eggs in early April, 6 of which hatched 61 days later. The newly hatched snakes are about 250 to 300 mm long. The adult Banded Krait reaches about 2m in length, and has been recorded to live for over $11\frac{1}{2}$ years in captivity.

Malayan Krait
Bungarus candidus

Venomous

This is a distinctly patterned snake of about 1 to 1.5 m long. Like all kraits, it is nocturnal and terrestrial in behaviour. During the day, the Malayan Krait spends its time hiding in holes or crevices in the ground. It feeds on other snakes and skinks, which it seizes and kills with its venomous bite. In captivity, it can be conditioned to accept dead prey. About 4 to 8 eggs are laid per clutch. These are said to be guarded by the female till they hatch. The Malayan Krait is fairly distributed, and inhabits hill forests.

Red-headed Krait
Bungarus flaviceps

Venomous

This beautiful snake is very similar to the Blue Coral Snake in coloration. However, the underside of the Red-headed Krait is white, but it is black in a young snake of the same species. It inhabits mountain and foothill forests, and is said to occur in coastal areas as well. Nothing much is known about its venom and thus it should be treated with respect. It seems to be rather rare. The adult Red-headed Krait is about 2 m long.

Genus Naja naja
(Indian Cobras)

We are all very familiar with the cobra's raised forebody and spectacularly outspread hood. This striking pose is further enhanced by the snake's hissing, and in some species, the spitting of venom at the eyes of its enemy. When the cobra is at rest, the hood is folded and hardly visible. There are about 10 recognised sub-species of cobras belonging to this genus, which occur in the Orient. Tweedie (1983) described 3 sub-species occurring in the Malaysian region, namely *Naja naja sputatrix*, *Naja naja kaouthia* and *Naja naja leucodira*.

Black Spitting Cobra spreads out its hood in an intimidating manner.

Black Spitting Cobra
Naja naja sputatrix

Venomous

This is a highly irascible, nocturnal snake with the alarming habit of spitting venom at the eyes of its molester, often with an uncanny accuracy involving distances of up to 2 m. The common sub-species is jet-black in colour, with a bluish black underside and some light-coloured markings on its throat. The Black Spitting Cobra grows to a length of about 1.5 m, and feeds on amphibians, reptiles, small mammals and birds. Though commonly found in the jungle, it also occurs in and near human settlements, where it does a good service by preying on rodent pests. It sometimes strays into gardens and houses when searching for food. When encountered, the cobra should be left strictly alone. Its bite, if left untreated, can have fatal consequences in about 1 to 6 hours.

Both sexes remain together during the

breeding season. The female Black Spitting Cobra lays between 6 and 20 eggs. On two occasions, a clutch of 7 eggs was laid in June, and another clutch of 7 eggs in early July. The eggs averaged 60.5 mm in length and 26 mm in diameter. It is said that both the parents stay together to brood the eggs. The incubation period is about 88 days. The newly hatched cobras are armed with fangs and venom glands. The Black Spitting Cobra is widely distributed in Singapore and Peninsular Malaysia. Another form of the Black Spitting Cobra, *Naja naja leucodira*, was described by Tweedie (1983) as sharing similar habitats with the *Naja naja sputatrix*.

Monocled Cobra
Naja naja kaouthia

Venomous

This is a lowland cobra that is easily recognised by its dorsal hood markings which consist of a whitish circle bordered with black. The circle usually encloses a dark spot, or sometimes up to 3 dark spots. The young of this sub-species may have dorsal crossbars which become obscure when they mature. Adult Monocled Cobras are about 1.4 m in length, and do not seem to be as irascible as the other species of cobras. Monocled Cobras occur in Thailand and are described by Tweedie to be found in the northern states of Peninsular Malaysia as well. Captive specimens have not been known to spit, though it is possible that they are able to do so. One 90-cm-long Monocled Cobra laid 9 eggs in late April, each egg averaging 52 mm in length and 26 mm in diameter. In the wild, this cobra is said to lay its eggs in a burrow and brood over them. The eggs hatch after an incubation period of 64 days. Monocled Cobras are widely distributed from Bangladesh to Indo-China and southeast China.

The Common Chinese Cobra is heavily-built and largely terrestrial

Head of Common Chinese Cobra

Common Chinese Cobra
Naja naja atra

Venomous

This heavily-built cobra occurs in south China, Taiwan, Indo-China, Thailand and Hong Kong. Owing to its wide geographical range, various colour forms have been described, ranging from yellow to dark brown. Some authorities have described certain races which are capable of spitting venom. However, the ones shown here, which are from Thailand, do not seem to have this defensive behaviour. Though capable of climbing, the Common Chinese Cobra is largely terrestrial, feeding on small prey, like birds, lizards and small mammals.

The breeding season is from February to March during which eggs numbering 9 to 14 are laid and brooded by the female snake. Each egg averages 50 mm in length and 25 mm in diameter, and weighs about 9 g. The incubation period is about 60 days, and the newly hatched baby cobras are about 280 mm long. In captivity, young Common Chinese Cobras feed readily on mice, chicks and garden lizards, and they attain maturity in about 3 years. The adult length is an impressive 1.5 m, and its venom is described as a potent neurotoxin.

Inset: The hood of the Philippine Cobra does not have any markings.

Philippine Cobra
Naja naja philippinensis

Venomous

This is one of the 3 sub-species of *Naja naja* found in the Philippine islands. The adult Phillipine Cobra is yellowish to olive brown with an underside that is yellowish white to cream in colour. There is no evidence of any other body markings in the adult Philippine Cobra though the young are dark brown to black with heavy reticulations of a light olive yellow in sharp contrast, and their underside is dirty, light olive in colour. The Philippine Cobra grows to about 1 m, and feeds on amphibians, other snakes and probably small mammals. About 12 eggs are laid per clutch, which hatch after an incubation period of about 49 days. Both the young and adult snakes possess potent venom and are said to probably cause more human deaths in the Philippines than any other venomous snake.

Genus Ophiophagus

King Cobra or Hamadryad
Ophiophagus hannah

Venomou[

This is reputed to be the largest venomous snake in the world, with a maximum recorded length of 6 m or so. The average length is less than this, being usually 3 to 4 m. Nevertheless, all King Cobras are formidable for their venom is a very potent neurotoxin. A bite from this cobra may prove to be rapidly fatal in half an hour or so. Even elephants have been known to die soon after being bitten by this snake. Death, when it occurs, mainly results from respiratory arrest and cardiac failure.

King Cobras occur throughout the region, being distributed in foothill jungles, open grasslands, rural areas and close to jungle streams. Though mainly terrestrial, it can climb fairly well. In captivity, King Cobras are often observed resting on branches and logs above the ground. Its diet comprises mainly other snakes, particularly rat snakes, though it has been known to take monitor lizards when in captivity. The prey is usually pursued, seized and killed by the cobra's deadly venom before being swallowed headfirst.

During the breeding season which is usually in April, the snakes exhibit seasonal monogamy. They are also the only snakes known to construct a nest of soil and vegetable debris in which they deposit their eggs. About 20 to 40 eggs are laid and brooded by the female till they hatch in 10 to 11 weeks. The hatchlings are about 50 cm long and are distinctly coloured. They are very precocious, and when disturbed, will rear up and spread out their hoods in an intimidating manner.

With the exception of man, adult King Cobras have hardly any natural enemies though there is an authentic case of an adult King Cobra being constricted to death by a Reticulated Python *(Python reticulatus)*.

The precocial baby King Cobra is fully armed with fangs and venom glands.

Opposite Page: The majestic King Cobra is a formidable animal to encounter in the field.

The Amphibious Sea Snake is partly land-bound as its eggs are deposited in rocky crevices.

Family Hydrophiidae (Sea Snakes)

The vast majority of snakes belonging to this family are entirely marine, and have special features, like flat, oar-shaped tails for swimming. Most of them spend their entire lives in the sea. Although being aquatic, sea snakes need to come up to the water surface to breathe once in a while, and will drown if deprived of the chance to do so.

All species, except *Laticauda*, produce live young. Sea snakes generally occur in shallow waters around the coast and river mouths as well as around islands. Some are pelagic and are found great distances away from land. All sea snakes are venomous, and they feed largely on fish, especially eels. Experiments have shown that the venom of some sea snakes is more potent than cobra venom. Fortunately, sea snakes are not outwardly aggressive and most bite cases are the result of rough handling or of the snakes being accidentally trodden upon by swimmers. Death can result from an untreated bite.

The family *Hydrophiidae* is represented by 16 genera with about 46 species distributed in the tropical seas of the world. About 22 species of sea snakes occur in the coastal areas of this region.

Amphibious Sea Snake
Laticauda colubrina

Venomous

This is a common sea snake of 1.2 m in length. It has not entirely severed its link with the land in the sense that it still retains large ventral scales, and can still move well over land. It reproduces by laying eggs instead of giving birth to live young, as is the case of the other species of marine snakes. Amphibious Sea Snakes have been observed to congregate in huge numbers on small, rocky islets and the surrounding sea during the breeding season. The eggs are deposited in crevices and holes in the rocks. The hatching of the eggs was reported to occur in the period of June to August on islands near Singapore. This snake is widely distributed, ranging from the Bay of Bengal to the southwestern part of the Pacific Ocean.

Head and tail of the Amphibious Sea Snake

Beak-like snout of the highly venomous Common Sea Snake

Common Sea Snake
Enhydrina schistosa

Venomous

This sea snake is distributed from the Persian Gulf, the Bay of Bengal, the Gulf of Thailand to the seas surrounding New Guinea and Australia. It is common in the western coastal areas of this region, and hence, is largely responsible for the numerous bites suffered by fisherfolk and swimmers. One prominent characteristic of this sea snake is the pronounced rostral scale on the tip of its upper lip, which gives it a beak-like appearance on its snout. Thus, it is sometimes known as the Beaked Sea Snake. Pregnant females are reported to occur in the period of December to February, and the number of young in a litter may range from 7 to 11. The Common Sea Snake grows to a length of 1 m, and its venom has been said to be the most toxic snake venom of all!

96

Adult and juvenile Hardwicke's Sea Snakes

Hardwicke's Sea Snake
Lapemis hardwickii

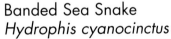

Venomous

This stout-bodied sea snake has a large head, which juxtaposes with its characteristically hexagonal or square scales. As with all sea snakes, the nostrils are upward-facing. The Hardwicke's Sea Snake feeds on fish and eels, and is very common in the coastal seas on both sides of Peninsular Malaysia as well as around islands. The height of the breeding season is from June to September, and it produces live young. Male Hardwicke's Sea Snakes have keeled scales on their bodies, whereas the females have smooth scales. Adults grow to 90 cm long.

Banded Sea Snake
Hydrophis cyanocinctus

Venomous

This is a widely distributed sea snake, occurring in the Persian Gulf, the Gulf of Thailand and the seas surrounding Japan and New Guinea. It is common in the coastal seas around Singapore and Peninsular Malaysia. Many variations in body colour and markings have been described, and this may be attributed to its wide geographical range. The scales on its body are moderately keeled. The Banded Sea Snake feeds on fish and eels, and grows to 2 m long. The venom is potently myotoxic.

Eyelash Sea Snake
Acalyptophis peronii

Venomous

This one-metre-long sea snake is so named because of the horn-like scaly projections on top of its eyes. It is a strikingly coloured sea snake occurring around the coastal regions of Australia, and has been recorded in the Gulf of Thailand. A specimen was collected by fishermen in the east coast of Peninsular Malaysia, and it is probable that future collections from this area may help to ascertain its occurrence in this part of the world. The Eyelash Sea Snake feeds on fish. Not much else is known about it.

Horn-like scaly projections above the eyes of the Eyelash Sea Snake

Olive Sea Snake
Praescutata viperina

Venomous

This widely distributed sea snake occurs in the Indian Ocean, the Straits of Malacca, the Gulf of Thailand and as far north as the seas surrounding Hong Kong. It also occurs in the seas around Indonesia and the Philippines. Two colour forms have been described, one of which is shown here. The other, a completely banded form, is said to occur in the Indian Ocean. Young Olive Sea Snakes are said to be banded. The breeding season of this sea snake in the Gulf of Thailand is reported to be in March and April. It produces live young, and one litter may number 3. The Olive Sea Snake grows to less than a metre long, and the usual length is between 75 and 90 cm.

Family Viperidae (Vipers)

This is a distinct group of venomous land snakes that possess long, moveable fangs in the front part of their upper jaws. All vipers generally have arrow-shaped heads, covered with numerous small scales except for the genus *Agkistrodon*. The head is distinct from the neck, and the body is stout in most species.

All the vipers occurring in this region belong to the sub-family *Crotalinae* or pit vipers. They are characterised by the presence of loreal pits between the nostrils and the eyes. These pits function as heat-seeking organs which help the snake to detect warm-blooded prey in the pitch darkness of the forest interior.

Two genera and 9 species of vipers occur in this region. Though all vipers are considered venomous, only some are regarded as deadly. Bites by many species usually cause extreme pain and swelling to the victim. An interesting behaviour observed in these vipers is their habit of tail-vibration when molested. This defensive action, when carried out amongst leaves, creates an audible rustling sound and serves to warn would-be predators that the snake is angry and likely to strike.

Arrow indicates position of loreal pit

The female coils itself on top of the eggs.

Genus Agkistrodon

This genus is distinguished from the other pit vipers found in this region by the large, symmetrically arranged scales on the head. The single species represented here also lays eggs instead of giving birth to live young.

Malayan Pit Viper
Agkistrodon rhodostoma

Venomous

The Malayan Pit Viper prefers drier habitats, and occurs in lowland areas, such as plantations and lowland forests. It is mainly terrestrial, often lying motionless among leaf litters to ambush unsuspecting prey, like mice, rats, shrews and squirrels. Its body colour and markings help it to merge almost perfectly into its natural habitat. It is highly irritable and will strike without warning: many people wearing inadequate footwear have been bitten when walking around in the snake's habitat. The eggs are laid in the period from June to September. A clutch may number from 13 to 30 eggs, and they measure, on the average, 29 mm in length and 19 mm in diameter. The female coils itself on top of the eggs, completely covering them till they hatch in 38 to 47 days. Newly hatched Malayan Pit Vipers are about 90 mm in length and have yellowish white tail tips. This snake grows to 60 cm long and is commonly found in the northern states of Peninsular Malaysia. It also occurs in Thailand and Sumatra.

Genus Trimeresurus

Pit vipers belonging to this genus have scales on their heads, which are all small and irregularly arranged. They bear live young instead of laying eggs. Of the 7 species occurring in the region of Singapore and Peninsular Malaysia, 4 are described here.

A young Wagler's Pit Viper

An adult Wagler's Pit Viper

Wagler's Pit Viper
Trimeresurus wagleri

Venomous

This snake is widely distributed in lowland and sub-montane jungles as well as in mangrove swamps. It may inhabit low shrubs or tall trees, where it spends its time coiled up motionless on a branch. Considered mild-mannered and not known to bite a human, the Wagler's Pit Viper is kept in big numbers in the Penang Snake Temple, where it is believed to bring good luck to the worshippers. In the wild, the Wagler's Pit Viper feeds on birds and jungle rats. A litter of up to 16 young are born. They are green with red and white spots along their backs. The adult grows to about 90 cm long, and though it is venomous, its bite is not deadly.

Sumatran Pit Viper
Trimeresurus sumatranus

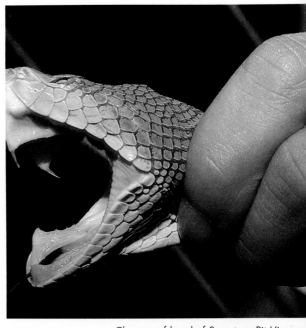

Venomous

The Sumatran Pit Viper grows to a length of about 1 m, and is largely arboreal by nature. Its venom fangs may be more than 10 mm long. It is fairly common in this region, inhabiting the forests, where the green colour of its body camouflages it among the branches and leaves. It looks somewhat similar to the Popes' Pit Viper except that the former is larger and its green tail is banded and tipped with red. The Sumatran Pit Viper does well in captivity, feeding on rats and mice.

Close-up of head of Sumatran Pit Viper, showing formidable sharp fangs.

The beautiful Popes' Pit Viper commonly occurs in montane forests.

Popes' Pit Viper
Trimeresurus popeiorum

Venomous

This is a slender-bodied, arboreal viper. This nocturnal viper commonly occurs in montane forests. It feeds on birds, frogs, lizards and squirrels. When molested, it will vibrate its tail, and is capable of inflicting a painful bite. Francis L.K. Lim was once bitten on the index finger by a 10-month-old Popes' Pit Viper, and immediately experienced piercing pain at the single puncture mark. Six hours after being bitten, the affected hand and whole arm had swelled to twice their normal size, and were tender to the touch. Nausea and much discomfort was felt. Complete recovery occurred 10 days after the accident. The breeding season seems to be in the first half of the year, as three females were each recorded to produce an average of 10 young in a litter between April and early May. The newborn vipers are about 178 mm long. When fully grown, the Popes' Pit Viper is about 90 cm long though the average length is about 60 cm.

Shore Pit Viper
Trimeresurus purpureomaculatus

Venomous

This viper commonly occurs in offshore islands and coastal mangrove swamps, and is sometimes called the Mangrove Pit Viper. It is said to be quite common in the mainland as well, and in Singapore, it has been captured in the Ponggol swamps and on Sentosa Island.

Largely arboreal, the Shore Pit Viper possesses a prehensile tail and spends much of its time coiled up in trees and shrubs where it ambushes small mammals and birds. In captivity, this viper will take mice and day-old chicks. Owing to its highly irritable nature, it will strike with little warning, and the consequences of its bite can be serious. Tail vibration has been observed when the snakes are disturbed.

Shore Pit Vipers are ovo-viviparous, and births in captivity of snakes from Thailand have been recorded in the months of April and May. In early May, one 60-cm-long Shore Pit Viper gave birth to 15 young, each averaging 24 cm in length. The young vipers are also highly irritable. They prey on house geckos, small frogs and mice.

Herpetologists have observed several colour variations in the Shore Pit Viper throughout its range in Southeast Asia, as clearly demonstrated by the specimens shown here. Its colour varies from blackish to dark purplishbrown, either uniform or variegated with pale green. Sometimes there is a white dotted line low down on each side of its body. Its belly is brown or greenish, and may be spotted with black. The adult Shore Pit Viper reaches a length of about 90 cm.

Shore Pit Viper from Singapore

Juvenile Shore Pit Viper

Shore Pit Viper from Peninsular Malaysia /Thailand

Appendix I

LIST OF SNAKES FOUND IN PENINSULAR MALAYSIA
(according to M.W.F. Tweedie, 1983)

Scientific Name	Common Name (where available)	Max. Length
Family Typhlopidae		
Ramphotyphlops braminus	Common Blind Snake	15 cm
Ranphotyphlops albiceps	White-headed Blind Snake	16 cm
Typhlops diardi muelleri	Diard's Blind Snake	40 cm
Typhlops lineatus	Striped Blind Snake	48 cm
Typhlops klemmeri		
Family Aniliidae		
Cylindrophis rufus	Red-tailed Pipe Snake	90 cm
Anomochilus leonardi	Leonard's Pipe Snake	22 cm
Family Xenopeltidae		
Xenopeltis unicolor	Iridescent Earth Snake	1 m
Family Boidae		
Python reticulatus	Reticulated Python	6 m
Python curtus	Blood Python	3 m
Family Acrochordidae		
Acrochordus javanicus	Elephant's Trunk Snake	2 m
Chersydrus granulatus	File Snake	1 m
Family Colubridae: Sub-family Pareinae		
Pareas vertebralis	Mountain Slug Snake	76 cm
Pareas laevis	Smooth Slug Snake	60 cm
Pareas carinatus	Keeled Slug Snake	60 cm
Pareas malaccanus	Malayan Slug Snake	
Pareas margaritophorus	White-spotted Slug Snake	30 cm
Aplopeltura boa	Blunt-headed Tree Snake	75 cm

Scientific Name	Common Name (where available)	Max. Length
Family Colubridae: Sub-family Xenodermatinae		
Xenodermus javanicus		65 cm
Family Colubridae: Sub-family Colubrinae		
Genera Elaphe, Gonyosoma	**Racers**	
Elaphe flavolineata	Common Racer	2 m
Elaphe taeniura	Striped Racer	2 m
Elaphe radiata	Copperhead Racer	2 m
Elaphe prasina	Green Tree Racer	1.5 m
Elaphe porphyracea	Red Mountain Racer	1 m
Gonyosoma oxycephalum	Red-tailed Racer	2 m
Genera Ptyas, Zaocys	**Rat Snakes**	
Ptyas korros	Indo-Chinese Rat Snake	2.2 m
Zaocys carinatus	Keeled Rat Snake	4 m
Zaocys fuscus	White-bellied Rat Snake	3 m
Genus Xenelaphis	**Brown Snakes**	
Xenelaphis hexagonotus	Malayan Brown Snake	2 m
Xenelaphis ellipsifer	Ocellated Brown Snake	3 m
Genus Liopeltis		
Liopeltis tricolor		50 cm
Liopeltis baliodeira		35 cm
Liopeltis longicauda		45 cm
Genus Oligodon	**Kukri Snakes**	
Oligodon octolineatus	Striped Kukri Snake	60 cm
Oligodon purpurascens	Brown Kukri Snake	80 cm
Oligodon signatus	Barred Kukri Snake	60 cm
Genera Calamaria, Pseudorhabdion, Collorhabdium, Macrocalamus, Oreocalamus	**Reed Snakes**	
Calamaria lumbricoidea	Variable Reed Snake	40 cm

Scientific Name	Common Name (where available)	Max. Length
Calamaria pavimentata	Collared Reed Snake	30 cm
Calamaria schlegeli schlegeli	Pink-headed Reed Snake	38 cm
Calamaria albiventer	Red-bellied Reed Snake	38 cm
Calamaria lowi gimletti	Gimlett's Reed Snake	20 cm
Pseudorhabdion longiceps	Dwarf Reed Snake	23 cm
Collorhabdium williamsoni	Williamson's Reed Snake	29 cm
Macrocalamus lateralis	Malayan Mountain Reed Snake	40 cm
Macrocalamus tweediei	Lim's Mountain Reed Snake	50 cm
Macrocalamus jasoni	Jason's Mountain Reed Snake	76 cm
Oreocalamus hanitschi	Hanitsch's Reed Snake	57 cm

Genus Dendrelaphis — Bronzebacks

Dendrelaphis pictus	Painted Bronzeback	1 m
Dendrelaphis formosus	Elegant Bronzeback	1 m
Dendrelaphis caudolineatus	Striped Bronzeback	1.5 m
Dendrelaphis striatus	Cohn's Bronzeback	not recorded

Genera Chrysopelea, Gonyophis — Tree Snakes

Chrysopelea paradisi	Paradise Tree Snake	1 m
Chrysopelea pelias	Twin-barred Tree Snake	65 cm
Chrysopelea ornata	Golden Tree Snake	1.3 m
Gonyophis margaritatus	Rainbow Tree Snake	1.7 m

Genera Lycodon, Lepturophis — Wolf Snakes

Lycodon aulicus	Common House or Wolf Snake	50 cm
Lycodon subcinctus	Banded Wolf Snake	1 m
Lycodon butleri	Butler's Wolf Snake	1 m
Lycodon effraenis	Scarce Wolf Snake	75 cm
Lycodon laoensis	Indo-Chinese Wolf Snake	45 cm
Lepturophis borneensis	Slender Wolf Snake	1.5 m

Genera Dryocalamus, Sibynophis

Dryocalamus subannulatus		50 cm
Sibynophis melanocephalus		60 cm
Sibynophis collaris		75 cm

Genus Boiga — Cat Snakes

Boiga dendrophila	Mangrove Snake	2.5 m

Scientific Name	Common Name (where available)	Max. Length
Boiga nigriceps	Dark-headed Cat Snake	1.5 m
Boiga jaspidea	Jasper Cat Snake	1 m
Boiga drapiezii	White-spotted Cat Snake	2 m
Boiga cynodon	Dog-toothed Cat Snake	2.5 m

Genus Psammodynastes
Mock Vipers

Psammodynastes pulverulentus	Mock Viper	60 cm
Psammodynastes pictus	Painted Mock Viper	50 cm

Genera Ahaetulla, Dryophiops
Whip Snakes

Ahaetulla prasina	Oriental Whip Snake	2 m
Ahaetulla mycterizan	Malayan Green Whip Snake	1 m
Ahaetulla fasciolata	Speckle-headed Whip Snake	1.5 m
Dryophiops rubescens	Keel-bellied Whip Snake	1 m

Family Colubridae: Sub-family Natricinae
Keelbacks

Natrix trianguligera	Triangle Keelback	1 m
Xenochrophis piscator	Chequered Keelback	1 m
Rhabdophis chrysargus	Speckle-bellied Keelback	80 cm
Rhabdophis subminiatus	Red-necked Keelback	80 cm
Macropophis maculatus	Spotted Keelback	80 cm
Amphiesma petersii	Peter's Keelback	60 cm
Amphiesma conspicillata	Red-bellied Keelback	38 cm
Amphiesma inas	Malayan Mountain Keelback	60 cm
Amphiesma sanguinea	Smedley's Keelback	60 cm
Amphiesma sarawacensis	Sarawak Mountain Keelback	60 cm
Pseudoxenodon macrops	Big-eyed Mountain Keelback	1.3 m
Macropisthodon rhodomelas	Blue-necked Keelback	45 cm
Macropisthodon flaviceps	Orange-necked Keelback	70 cm

Family Colubridae: Sub-family Homalopsinae
Water Snakes

Enhydris enhydris		60 cm
Enhydris plumbea		40 cm
Enhydris punctata		40 cm

Scientific Name	Common Name (where available)	Max. Length
Enhydris pahangensis		22 cm
Enhydris bocourti	Bocourt's Water Snake	1 m
Enhydris indica		47 cm
Homalopsis buccata	Puff-faced Water Snake	1.2 m
Cerberus rhynchops	Dog-faced Water Snake	1 m
Gerardia prevostiana	Gerard's Water Snake	50 cm
Fordonia leucobalia	Crab-eating Water Snake	1 m
Cantoria violacea	Cantor's Water Snake	1 m
Bitia hydroides	Keel-bellied Water Snake	45 cm

Family Elapidae
Genus Bungarus — **Kraits**

Bungarus fasciatus	Banded Krait	2 m
Bungarus candidus	Malayan Krait	1 m
Bungarus flaviceps	Red-headed Krait	2 m

Genera Calliophis, Maticora — **Coral Snakes**

Calliophis gracilis	Spotted Coral Snake	65 cm
Calliophis maculiceps	Small-spotted Coral Snake	45 cm
Maticora bivirgata	Blue Malayan Coral Snake	1.5 m
Maticora intestinalis	Banded Malayan Coral Snake	50 cm

Genera Naja, Ophiophagus — **Cobras**

Naja naja	Indian Cobra	2 m
Ophiophagus hannah	Hamadryad or King Cobra	4.5 m

Family Hydrophiidae — **Sea Snakes**

Laticauda colubrina	Amphibious Sea Snake	1.4 m
Aipysurus eydouxii		1 m
Kerilia jerdoni		1 m
Praescutata viperina		1 m
Enhydrina schistosa	Beaked Sea Snake	1.4 m
Hydrophis klossi		1.3 m
Hydrophis cyanocinctus		2 m
Hydrophis spiralis		2 m
Hydrophis melanosoma		1.5 m
Hydrophis caerulescens		80 cm

Scientific Name	Common Name (where available)	Max. Length
Hydrophis ornatus		1 m
Hydrophis torquatus torquatus		80 cm
Hydrophis torquatus aagardi		90 cm
Hydrophis brookii		1 m
Hydrophis fasciatus fasciatus		1 m
Hydrophis fasciatus atriceps		not recorded
Thalassophis anomalus		80 cm
Kolpophis annandalei		90 cm
Lapemis hardwickii		90 cm
Astrotia stokesii		2 m
Microcephalophis gracilis		1 m
Pelamis platurus	Yellow-bellied Sea Snake	1 m

Family Viperidae
Genus Agkistrodon

Pit Vipers

Agkistrodon rhodostoma	Malayan Pit Viper	80 cm

Genus Trimeresurus

Trimeresurus wagleri	Wagler's Pit Viper	1 m
Trimeresurus sumatranus	Sumatran Pit Viper	1 m
Trimeresurus hageni	Hagen's Pit Viper	not recorded
Trimeresurus popeiorum	Popes' Pit Viper	1 m
Trimeresurus monticola	Mountain Pit Viper	1 m
Trimeresurus purpureomaculatus	Shore Pit Viper	1 m
Trimeresurus puniceus	Flat-nosed Pit Viper	60 cm

Appendix II
DISTRIBUTION CHART & LIST OF COMMON NAMES
OF SNAKES OF SOUTHEAST ASIA

Common Name	Scientific Name	Page No.	Singapore	Pen. Malaysia	Thailand	Philippines	Borneo	Sumatra	Java
Amphibious Sea Snake	*Laticauda colubrina*	95	✔	✔	✔		✔	✔	✔
Banded Coral Snake	*Maticora intestinalis*	84	✔	✔	✔	✔	✔	✔	✔
Banded Krait	*Bungarus fasciatus*	85	✔	✔	✔		✔	✔	✔
Banded Rat Snake	*Ptyas mucosus*	44	(✔)*		✔		✔	✔	
Banded Sea Snake	*Hydrophis cyanocinctus*	97	✔	✔	✔	✔			✔
Black-headed Collared Snake	*Sibynophis melanocephalus*	57	✔	✔			✔	✔	✔
Black Spitting Cobra	*Naja naja sputatrix*	88	✔	✔					
Blood Python	*Python curtus*	27	(✔)	✔	✔		✔	✔	
Blue Coral Snake	*Maticora bivirgata*	83	✔	✔	✔	✔	✔	✔	✔
Blue-necked Keelback	*Macropisthodon rhodomelas*	61	✔	✔			✔	✔	✔
Bocourt's Water Snake	*Enhydris bocourti*	72		✔	✔				
Brown Kukri Snake	*Oligodon purpurascens*	47	✔	✔	✔		✔	✔	✔
Chequered Keelback	*Xenochrophis piscator*	58	(✔)	✔	✔	✔	✔	✔	✔
Common Blind Snake	*Ramphotyphlops braminus*	30	✔	✔	✔	✔	✔	✔	✔
Common Chinese Cobra	*Naja naja atra*	90			✔				
Common House or Wolf Snake	*Lycodon aulicus*	54	✔	✔	✔	✔	✔	✔	✔
Common Racer	*Elaphe flavolineata*	38	✔	✔	✔		✔	✔	✔
Common Sea Snake	*Enhydrina schistosa*	96	✔	✔	✔	✔	✔		
Copperhead Racer	*Elaphe radiata*	39	✔	✔	✔		✔	✔	✔
Diard's Blind Snake	*Typhlops diardi muelleri*	31	✔	✔	✔		✔	✔	
Dog-faced Water Snake	*Cerberus rhynchops*	71	✔	✔	✔	✔	✔		✔
Dog-toothed Cat Snake	*Boiga cynodon*	78	✔	✔	✔		✔	✔	✔
Dwarf Reed Snake	*Pseudorhabdion longiceps*	50	✔	✔			✔	✔	
Elegant Bronzeback	*Dendrelaphis formosus*	53	✔	✔	✔		✔	✔	✔
Elephant's Trunk Snake	*Acrochordus javanicus*	34	(✔)	✔	✔		✔	✔	✔
Eyelash Sea Snake	*Acalyptophis peronii*	98		✔	✔				
File Snake	*Chersydrus granulatus*	35	✔	✔	✔		✔	✔	✔

* Present status uncertain or unconfirmed

Common Name	Scientific Name	Page No.	Singapore	Pen. Malaysia	Thailand	Philippines	Borneo	Sumatra	Java
Golden Tree Snake	*Chrysopelea ornata*	64		✔	✔	✔	✔	✔	
Green Cat-eyed Snake	*Boiga cyanea*	81		✔	✔				
Hardwicke's Sea Snake	*Lapemis hardwickii*	97	✔	✔	✔	✔	✔		✔
Indo-Chinese Rat Snake	*Ptyas korros*	43	✔	✔	✔	✔	✔	✔	✔
Indo-Chinese Wolf Snake	*Lycodon laoensis*	56		✔	✔				
Iridescent Earth Snake	*Xenopeltis unicolor*	33	✔	✔	✔		✔	✔	✔
Jasper Cat Snake	*Boiga jaspidea*	79	✔	✔			✔	✔	✔
Keel-bellied Whip Snake	*Dryophiops rubescens*	69	✔	✔	✔		✔	✔	✔
Keeled Rat Snake	*Zaocys carinatus*	42	✔	✔			✔	✔	✔
Keeled Slug Snake	*Pareas carinatus*	37		✔			✔	✔	✔
King Cobra	*Ophiophagus hannah*	92	✔	✔	✔	✔	✔	✔	✔
Long-nosed Whip Snake	*Ahaetulla nasuta*	68		✔					
Malayan Brown Snake	*Xenelaphis hexagonotus*	45	✔	✔	✔		✔	✔	✔
Malayan Krait	*Bungarus candidus*	86	✔	✔	✔			✔	✔
Malayan Pit Viper	*Agkistrodon rhodostoma*	101		✔	✔			✔	✔
Mangrove Snake	*Boiga dendrophila melanota*	76	✔	✔			✔	✔	✔
Mock Viper	*Psammodynastes pulverulentus*	75		✔	✔	✔	✔	✔	✔
Monocled Cobra	*Naja naja kaouthia*	89		✔	✔				
Olive Sea Snake	*Praescutata viperina*	99	✔	✔	✔	✔	✔		✔
Orange-bellied Snake	*Liopeltis baliodeira*	51	✔	✔			✔	✔	✔
Oriental Whip Snake	*Ahaetulla prasina*	67	✔	✔	✔		✔	✔	✔
Painted Bronzeback	*Dendrelaphis pictus*	52	✔	✔	✔		✔	✔	✔
Paradise Tree Snake	*Chrysopelea paradisi*	62	✔	✔		✔	✔	✔	✔
Philippine Cobra	*Naja naja philippinensis*	91				✔			
Pink-headed Reed Snake	*Calamaria schlegeli schlegeli*	49	✔	✔			✔	✔	
Plumbeous Water Snake	*Enhydris plumbea*	73	(✔)*	✔	✔		✔	✔	✔
Popes' Pit Viper	*Trimeresurus popeiorum*	105		✔	✔		✔	✔	
Puff-faced Water Snake	*Homalopsis buccata*	71	✔	✔	✔		✔	✔	✔
Rainbow Water Snake	*Enhydris enhydris*	73	(✔)	✔	✔		✔	✔	✔
Red-headed Krait	*Bungarus flaviceps*	87		✔	✔		✔	✔	✔

* Present status uncertain or unconfirmed

Common Name	Scientific Name	Page No.	Singapore	Pen. Malaysia	Thailand	Philippines	Borneo	Sumatra	Java
Red-necked Keelback	Rhabdophis subminiatus	60	(✔)*	✔	✔				
Red-tailed Pipe Snake	Cylindrophis rufus	32	✔	✔	✔		✔	✔	✔
Red-tailed Racer	Gonyosoma oxycephalum	41	✔	✔	✔	✔	✔	✔	✔
Reticulated Python	Python reticulatus	26	✔	✔	✔	✔	✔	✔	✔
Rock Python	Python molurus bivittatus	28			✔				
Scarce Wolf Snake	Lycodon effraenis	55		✔			✔	✔	
Shore Pit Viper	Trimeresurus purpureomaculatus	106	✔	✔				✔	
Striped Bronzeback	Dendrelaphis caudolineatus	53	✔	✔	✔	✔	✔	✔	
Striped Keelback	Xenochrophis vittatus	59	(✔)					✔	✔
Striped Kukri Snake	Oligodon octolineatus	47	✔	✔			✔	✔	✔
Striped Racer	Elaphe taeniura	40	(✔)	✔	✔		✔	✔	
Sumatran Pit Viper	Trimeresurus sumatranus	103	(✔)	✔			✔	✔	
Tentacled Snake	Herpeton tentaculatum	74			✔				
Twin-barred Tree Snake	Chrysopelea pelias	65	✔	✔			✔	✔	
Variable Reed Snake	Calamaria lumbricoidea	48	✔	✔		✔	✔	✔	✔
Wagler's Pit Viper	Trimeresurus wagleri	102	✔	✔	✔	✔	✔	✔	
White-spotted Cat Snake	Boiga drapiezii	77	(✔)	✔			✔	✔	✔

* Present status uncertain or unconfirmed

Bibliography

Ambu, Stephen & Lim, Boo Liat (1988) "A study of snake-bites in Peninsular Malaysia with special reference to Perlis & Kedah from 1979-1983". *Tropical Biomedicine 5: 65–67.*

Boulenger, George A. (1912) *A Vertebrate Fauna of the Malay Peninsular — Reptilia and Batrachia.* Federated Malay States Government Press, Kuala Lumpur, Malaysia.

Fitch, Henry S. (1970) *Reproductive Cycles of Lizards and Snakes.* University of Kansas Printing Service, Lawrence, Kansas, U.S.A.

Griehl, Klaus (1984) *Snakes* (First English Language Edition). Barrens Educational Series Inc., 113 Crossways Park Drive, Woodbury, New York, U.S.A.

Grzimek, Bernhard (1975) "Reptiles". *Grzimek's Animal Life Encyclopedia, Vol 6.* Van Nostrand Reinhold Co., New York, London, Melbourne.

Kuntz, Robert E. (Cpt.) (1977) *Snakes of Taiwan.* United States Naval Medical Research Unit No. 2, Taipei, Taiwan.

Lim, Boo Liat (1970) "Bites and Stings by Venomous Animals with Special Reference to Snake Bites in West Malaysia". *The Medical Journal of Malaya, Vol 25, No. 2.*

Lim, Boo Liat (1979) *Poisonous Snakes of Peninsular Malaysia,* 1st. Edition. Malayan Nature Society, Kuala Lumpur, Malaysia.

Lim, Boo Liat (1982) *Poisonous Snakes of Peninsular Malaysia,* 2nd. Edition. Malayan Nature Society, Kuala Lumpur, Malaysia.

Lim, Francis L.K. (1980) "The Husbandry and Reproduction of the Mangrove Snake" (*Boiga dendrophila*), ZOOM-80. Singapore Zoological Gardens.

Lim, Francis L.K. (1980) "The Mangrove Snake". *Nature Malaysiana, Vol 5, No. 4.* Tropical Press Sdn. Bhd., Kuala Lumpur, Malaysia.

Lim, Francis L.K. (1981) "The Reticulated Python". *Nature Malaysiana, Vol 6, No. 4,* Tropical Press Sdn. Bhd., Kuala Lumpur, Malaysia.

Pelton, Robert W. & Carden, Karen W. (1979) *Snake Handlers — God-fearers or Fanatics?* Thomas Nelson Inc., Nashville, Tennessee, U.S.A.

Phleps, Tony (1981) *Poisonous Snakes.* Blandford Press Ltd Link House, West Street, U.K.

Porter, Kenneth R. (1972) *Herpetology.* W.B. Saunders Company, Philadelphia, London, Toronto

Ram, Panjabi (1976) "To have Confronted the Cobra — even in Worship…" *The Asia Magazine,* December 26, 1976: 30-32.

Reid, H.A. (1963) "Epidemiology of Snake Bites in North Malaya". *British Medical Journal:* 992–997.

Reitinger, Frank F. (1978) *Common Snakes of South-east Asia and Hong Kong*. Heinemann Educational Books (Asia) Ltd.

Stidworthy, John (1969) *Snakes of the World*. The Hamlyn Publishing Group Ltd., London, New York, Sydney, Toronto.

Taylor, Edward H. (1922) *The Snakes of the Philippine Islands*, Publication No. 16, 1922.

Teo, S.K. (1982) "A Review of Snake Bites treated at Changi Hospital". *The Singapore Family Physician, Vol VIII, No. 3, July/September*: 72. The College of General Practitioners Singapore.

Tweedie, M.W.F. (1961) *The Snakes of Malaya*, 2nd edition. Government Printing Office, Singapore.

Tweedie, M.W.F. (1983) *The Snakes of Malaya*, 3rd edition. Singapore National Printers (Pte) Ltd., Singapore.

Whitaker, Romulus (1978) *Common Indian Snakes*. Macmillan India Ltd. Delhi, Bombay, Calcutta, Madras.

Index

Acalyptophis peronii   98
Acrochordidae   34
Acrochordus javanicus   34
Adrenaline   21. *See also* Antivenin
Agkistrodon   100
    rhodostoma   101
Ahaetulla
    nasuta   68
    prasina   67
Amoebic dysentry   2
Amphibious Sea Snake   95
Anaconda   1, 23
Analgesic   19, 20
Anaphylactic shock   21. *See also* Snakebite,
        treatment of
Aniliidae   32
Antidote   15, 17
Antihistamine   21
Antiseptic   19
Antivenin
    specific   20
    polyvalent   20
    administration of   21
    dosage of   21
Artificial respiration   20

Banded Coral Snake   84
Banded Krait   76, 85
Banded Rat Snake   44
Banded Sea Snake   97
Beaked Sea Snake. *See* Common Sea Snake
Black-headed Collared Snake   57
Black Spitting Cobra   10, 19, 88-89
Blind snakes   30-31
Blood Python   27
Blue Coral Snake   14, 83, 87
Blue-necked Keelback   61
Boas   26
Boa constrictor   2
Bocourt's Water Snake   72
Boidae   26

Boiga
    cyanea   81
    cynodon   78
    dendrophila melanota   76
    drapiezii   77
    jaspidea   79
Bronzebacks   52-53
Brown Kukri Snake   46, 47
Brown snakes   45
Bungarus
    candidus   86
    fasciatus   76, 85
    flaviceps   87

Calamaria
    lumbricoidea   48
    schlegeli schlegeli   49
Cat snakes   76-81
Cerberus rhynchops   71
Chequered Keelback   58, 60
Chersydrus granulatus   35
Chrysopelea
    ornata   64
    paradisi   62
    pelias   65
Cobras   88-91
Collared Snakes   57
Colubridae   36
Colubrinae   38
Colubrine snakes   36, 58
Common Blind Snake   30, 84
Common Chinese Cobra   90
Common House or Wolf Snake   9, 54
Common Racer   38
Common Sea Snake   96
Constrictor constrictor   2
Copperhead Racer   39
Coral snakes   82-84
Crotalinae   100
Cylindrophis rufus   32
Cytotoxic   22

Dendrelaphis
  caudolineatus 53
  formosus 53
  pictus 52
Diard's Blind Snake 31
Dog-faced Water Snake 71
Dog-toothed Cat Snake 78
Dryophiops rubescens 69
Dwarf Blind Snake 23
Dwarf Reed Snake 50

Earth snakes 33
Elaphe
  flavolineata 38
  radiata 39
  taeniura 40
Elapidae 82
Elapids 22
Elegant Bronzeback 53
Elephant's Trunk Snake 34
Enhydrina schistosa 96
Enhydris
  bocourti 72
  enhydris 73
  plumbea 73
Enteritis 2
Eunectes murinus 1, 23
Eyelash Sea Snake 98

First Aid 18
File Snake 35
Flying snakes 62-6

Geckos 3, 106
Golden Tree Snake 64
Gonyosoma oxycephalum 41
Grass snakes. *See* Keelbacks 58
Green Cat-eyed Snake 81

Haemoglobinuria 22
Haemotoxic 22
Hamadryad 24, 92

Hardwicke's Sea Snake 97
Herpetologists 1, 2, 23, 28, 106
Herpeton tentaculatum 74
Homalopsinae 70
Homalopsis buccata 71
Hydrocortisone 21
Hydrophiidae 94
Hydrophis cyanocinctus 97
Hyperkalemia 22
Hypertension 7
Hypodermic syringe 82

Indian Cobra 5, 10, 88
Indo-Chinese Rat Snake 43
Indo-Chinese Wolf Snake 56
Iridescent Earth Snake 33

Jacobson's organs 25
Jasper Cat Snake 79

Keelbacks 58-61
Keel-bellied Whip Snake 69
Keeled Rat Snake 42
Keeled Slug Snake 37
King Cobra 10, 24, 92
Kraits 85-87
Kukris 46-47

Lapemis hardwickii 97
Laticauda 94
  colubrina 95
Leptotyphlops humilis 23
Liopeltis baliodeira 51
Longevity 1-2
Long-nosed Whip Snake 68
Lycodon
  aulicus 54
  effraenis 55
  laoensis 56

Macropisthodon rhodomelas 61
Malayan Brown Snake 45

Malayan Krait   86
Malayan Pit Viper   8, 10, 13, 101
Mangrove Snake   76
Maticora
    bivirgata   83
    intestinalis   84
Mock Viper   75
Monocled Cobra   89
Mouth rot   2
Myoglobinuria   22
Myotoxic   22, 97

Naja naja   88
    atra   90
    kaouthia   88, 89
    leucodira   88
    philippinensis   91
    sputatrix   88
Natricinae   58
Nausea   105
Neurotoxic   22
Neurotoxin   85, 92

Ocellated Brown Snake   45
Oligodon
    octolineatus   47
    purpurascens   47
Olive Sea Snake   99
Ophiophagus hannah   92
Orange-bellied Snake   51
Oriental Whip Snake   24, 67, 81

Painted Bronzeback   52, 53
Paracetamol   20
Paradise Tree Snake   62
Parasitic worm   2
Pareas carinatus   37
Pareinae   36
Philippine Cobra   91
Pink-headed Reed Snake   49
Pipe snakes   32
Plumbeous Water Snake   73

Pneumonia   2
Popes' Pit Viper   104, 105
Praescutata viperina   99
Psammodynastes pulverulentus   75
Pseudorhabdion longiceps   50
Ptyas
    korros   43
    mucosus   44
Puff-faced Water Snake   70
Pythons   2-3, 6, 9, 12, 26-29
Python
    curtus   27
    molurus bivittatus   2, 28
    reticulatus   23, 26-27, 92

Racers   38-41
Rainbow Water Snake   73
Ramphotyphlops braminus   30
Rat snakes   42-44
Rattlesnake   5
Red-headed Krait   87
Red-necked Keelback   60, 61
Red-tailed Pipe Snake   32
Red-tailed Racer   41
Reed snakes   48-50
Religion and folklore   4-7
Reptile medicine   2
Reticulated python   3, 23, 92
Rhabdophis subminiatus   60
Rheumatism   7
Rock Python   3, 28-29

Scarce Wolf Snake   55
Sea snakes   94-99
Shore Pit Viper   10, 106
Short Python. *See* Blood Python
Sibynophis melanocephalus   57
Slug snakes   36
Snakebites   7, 13-15
    prevention of   16-17
    treatment of   17-20
Snake charmer   6-7

Snake encounter   8-10
Snake feeding
    feeding times   3
    food preferences   1
Snake hooks   9, 11-12
Snake-keeping   2-3
Snake temple   6, 102
Striped Bronzeback   53
Striped Keelback   59
Striped Kukri Snake   47
Striped Racer   40
Strychnine   5
Sumatran Pit Viper   103

Tentacled Snake   74
Tourniquet   19-21
Trimeresurus
    popeiorum   105
    purpureomaculatus   106
    sumatranus   103
    wagleri   102
Tuberculosis   2
Twin-barred Tree Snake   65
Typhlopidae   30

Typhlops diardi muelleri   31

Variable Reed Snake   48
Venom, types of   22
Vipers   100-107
Viperidae   100

Wagler's Pit Viper   6, 102
Water Snake. See *Acrochordidae, Homalopsinae, Herpeton*
Whip snakes   66-69
White-spotted Cat Snake   77
Wolf snakes   54-57

Xenelaphis
    ellipsifer   45
    hexagonotus   45
Xenochrophis
    piscator   58, 60
    vittatus   59
Xenopeltis unicolor   33

Zaocys carinatus   42

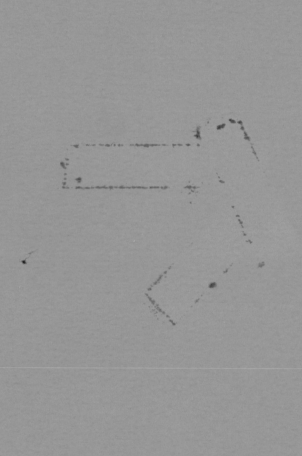